SACAGAWEA
SHOSHONE EXPLORER

SHAPERS OF AMERICA

SACAGAWEA
SHOSHONE EXPLORER

MICHAEL T. CROSBY

OTIN
PUBLISHING
STOCKTON, NJ

Frontispiece: Although no images of Sacagawea were made in her lifetime, she has been depicted in more statues than any other woman in American history. This 1980 painted bronze statue by Harry Jackson can be found at the Buffalo Bill Historical Center in Cody, Wyoming.

OTTN Publishing
16 Risler Street
Stockton, NJ 08859
www.ottnpublishing.com

First printing

1 3 5 7 9 8 6 4 2

Library of Congress Cataloging-in-Publication Data

Crosby, Michael T.
  Sacagawea : Shoshone Explorer / Michael T. Crosby.
      p. cm. — (Shapers of America)
  Includes bibliographical references and index.
  ISBN-13: 978-1-59556-026-1
  ISBN-10: 1-59556-026-2
  1. Sacagawea—Juvenile literature. 2. Lewis and Clark Expedition
(1804-1806)—Juvenile literature. 3. Shoshoni
women—Biography—Juvenile literature. 4. Shoshoni
Indians—Biography—Juvenile literature. 5. West
(U.S.)—Biography—Juvenile literature. I. Title.
  F592.7.S123C76 2008
  978'.004974'0092—dc22
  [B]
                                        2007024698

Editor's Note: The words reproduced from the expedition journals contain many misspelled words, or grammatical errors given as phonetic spellings, that were typical of the time. The entries appear as originally published.

Publisher's Note: The Web sites listed in this book were active at the time of publication. The publisher is not responsible for Web sites that have changed their address or discontinued operation since the date of publication. The publisher reviews and updates the Web sites each time the book is reprinted.

TABLE OF CONTENTS

SHAPERS OF AMERICA

INTRODUCTION

BY DR. ROGER G. KENNEDY

The SHAPERS OF AMERICA series profiles men and women who have had a powerful effect on the way our country has evolved. The subjects of these biographies were selected because their lives are interesting and important, and because they show what people like us can do when we summon the courage and persistence to make history. We may admire the subjects of these biographies, but their achievements, while great, are not so great as to seem irrelevant or inaccessible to our own lives.

The books in this series are not about celebrity, but about citizenship. One criterion for selection into the series is that the subjects of these biographies are not as well known as they should be. We all know something about George Washington, Thomas Jefferson, Abraham Lincoln, and Theodore Roosevelt. But over more than two centuries many other Americans have also made indelible contributions to the future of their nation and our world. The people profiled in the SHAPERS OF AMERICA series are not likely to be sculpted onto another Mount Rushmore. However, their lives affirm an inquiring and active citizenship—a citizenship that wants to know, and is willing to venture into the unknown for good purpose.

Dr. Roger G. Kennedy is the former director of the National Park Service and is director emeritus of the National Museum of American History in Washington, D.C.

I want to comment on something that has become important to me over more than sixty years in public life: although the men and women profiled in this series changed history, they were not set apart from the rest of us by knowing in advance the exact outcome of their actions. Sometimes things turned out as they intended, sometimes not. But as the old Southern expression goes, they put down their buckets where they were, drew up the water of life, and drank deep. They acted on the best information they could get—in many cases, amid much confusion and dispute—as we all must.

Striving amid doubt, each of them could take as a text a statement made in the midst of the Civil War by Abraham Lincoln: "I do the very best I know how—the very best I can; and I mean to keep on doing that until the end. If the end brings me out all right, then what is said against me won't amount to anything. If the end brings me out wrong, 10,000 angels swearing I was right would make no difference."

The biographies of the SHAPERS OF AMERICA series reveal people who used their talents and adapted to their circumstances in order to accomplish the extraordinary. None of the people in these volumes were perfect. Each got things wrong from time to time. But they put down their buckets where they were, and kept on trying their best despite derision and defeat. That is why they can be exemplars. They were capable of acting together with others to make matters better.

Acting together! That's the key to it! Benjamin Franklin's Poor Richard said: "He that drinks his cider alone, let him catch his horse alone." There never was a lone cowboy capable of much—or very happy for very long. "He who can be happy alone," said Aristotle, "is either a brute or a God." We are citizens. The same Founding

Fathers who wrote of the pursuit of happiness—without making any promise of finding it—wrote of seeking "a *more perfect* union." They did not proclaim that their new American nation was perfect; they left plenty of room for the work of the rest of us—including the work of the people in these books.

A more perfect union comes about in increments, as each generation engages in the pursuit of happiness. The lives profiled in the SHAPERS OF AMERICA series can inspir-it us to renew our own energies and to assert an active pursuit of happiness through public service. The true reward of citizenship comes from doing the best you can with what you've got, working together with—and for—other people. Putting your talents to use for the common good is a grand kind of happiness.

WHO WAS SACAGAWEA?

The crowd bustled around the huge American flag-draped statue expectantly, waiting for its unveiling. It was July 6, 1905, and the United States was celebrating the 100-year anniversary of the Lewis and Clark Expedition—a journey of exploration led by Captains Meriwether Lewis and William Clark through the American West that took place in the early 1800s. Now, a century later, at a special exposition in Portland, Oregon, the audience listened to several speeches commemorating the actions of a special member of the expedition—a Shoshone woman known as Sacagawea.

This bronze statue of Sacagawea, by Alice Cooper, was the first sculpture in the United States to honor the only woman in the Lewis and Clark Expedition. Unveiled in 1905 at the Lewis and Clark Exposition in Portland, Oregon, the statue was commissioned and paid for by donations from women's groups across the nation. It stands today in the city's Washington Park.

Sacagawea had been the only woman in the Corps of Discovery, as the Lewis and Clark Expedition was also known. She was just 17 and already a wife and mother of an infant son when she joined her husband, Toussaint Charbonneau, on the long journey of exploration with the Corps. During that journey, she assumed many roles. She was a translator, helping Lewis and Clark communicate with various Native American tribes. She was a guide, showing the way as the Corps traveled through her homeland. And she was a teacher, explaining the culture of her land and its people.

A POWERFUL SYMBOL

One hundred years after the William and Clark Expedition, Sacagawea had become something else—a powerful symbol of a woman's right to equal treatment in society. Suffragettes pointed to Sacagawea as someone who had been granted a right that women a century later were still struggling to achieve—the right to vote. That is why, in 1905, many women activists came to the Lewis and Clark Exposition in Portland to pay tribute to a historical moment and person.

The Lewis and Clark Expedition

William Clark and Meriwether Lewis were tasked in the early 1800s by President Thomas Jefferson with exploring the wilderness of the American Northwest. During the Lewis and Clark Expedition, its leaders made detailed records of hundreds of birds, plants, fish, and animals previously unknown to people living east of the Mississippi River.

The Portland exposition took place on land about 90 miles away from the site of a winter fort built by the Corps of Discovery. In December 1805, after spending several cold, miserable weeks camped on various spots along the north side of the Columbia River, the expedition had moved to the south side of the river as the result of a historic vote. Lewis and Clark had included each member of their group in making the decision on where to base their winter quarters. Among those participating in the vote were Clark's African-American slave York and Sacagawea, a Native American.

The decision to include York and Sacagawea in a vote was unusual for the time, to say the least. In the early 19th century, most African Americans were slaves with few rights; blacks were not permitted to vote in national elections. Women in American society were typically discouraged from giving their opinions and also could not vote in political elections. But on November 24, 1805, Lewis and Clark counted both Sacagawea's and York's votes equally with those of the other members of the expedition.

In the early 20th century, the story of Sacagawea's vote served as a great inspiration to leaders of the women's rights movement. As they actively campaigned for a woman's right to vote, they asked how their country could deny this essential right of equality a century after Sacagawea had exercised the franchise.

Susan B. Anthony (1820–1906), a social reformer who devoted her life to such causes as the abolition of slavery and equal rights for women, spoke before the unveiling of Sacagawea's statue at the Lewis and Clark Exposition in Portland. In her speech, she focused on Sacagawea's actions during her time with the Corps as an example of the patriotic role that women have played in American history:

Suffragist Susan B. Anthony (1820–1906) was a longtime activist for the woman's right to vote. In her 1905 speech at the dedication of the statue of Sacagawea, she described the Shoshone woman as a "patriot," whose efforts helped build the United States.

"This is the first time in history that a statue has been erected in the memory of a woman who has accomplished patriotic deeds," Anthony stated. "[If] it were not for that brave little Indian mother, there would be no Oregon or Portland."

Sacagawea was indeed brave, but it is unlikely that she viewed her contributions to the Lewis and Clark Expedition as "patriotic deeds." It is difficult to characterize her as a patriot when according to the laws at the time she was not even recognized as a U.S. citizen. Anthony's remarks were an example of how the historical Sacagawea had become lost, replaced in 1905 by the stereotype of a patient and wise Native American woman who guided the way for American westward expansion.

At the end of the speeches, the huge flag was pulled off the bronze statue, and the crowd broke into cheers. The sculpture was of a young Shoshone woman with her infant son strapped to her back. Wearing a brave, determined expression, the figure representing Sacagawea pointed dramatically to the West.

THE REAL SACAGAWEA

So who was the real Sacagawea? Despite her importance to American history, there is remarkably little reliable information available about the woman who served as the guide and interpreter for the Lewis and Clark Expedition. No portraits were ever painted of her, so her actual appearance remains unknown. No written records exist to verify her date of birth or death. People cannot even agree about the proper spelling of her name.

Most of what is definitively known about Sacagawea comes from journals written by members of the Corps of Discovery during their journey from St. Louis, Missouri, to the Pacific Ocean and back. However, the authors of

In addition to Captains Lewis and Clark, several members of the expedition kept journals documenting the experiences of the Corps of Discovery. They included soldier John Ordway, from New Hampshire; Patrick Gass, a carpenter from Pennsylvania; and Joseph Whitehouse, a tailor from Virginia. In the journals, Sacagawea is referred to by name, as "the interpreter's wife," and as the "Squar" or "Squaw"—a term that whites at the time thought was the Indian word for "wife" or "woman."

What's in a Name?

Is it *Sacagawea*, *Sacajawea*, or *Sakakawea*? The spelling, pronunciation, and meaning of Sacagawea's name is quite controversial. Lewis and Clark used variations of *Sah-ca-gah-we-a* and *Sah-kah-gar-we-a* in the journals they kept. In all cases, the third syllable of the name always started with a *g*. However, in the first edition of Lewis and Clark's journal, published in 1814, the name appears as Sacajawea, with a *j*. To add to the confusion, in a list of the Corps made by Clark in the 1820s, he wrote *Se car ja we au*.

Sacagawea lived with two different Native American tribes—the Shoshone and the Hidatsa. She had been living with the Hidatsa people when she joined the expedition, and William and Clark thought her name was Hidatsa for "Bird Woman," or *tsakaka wia*. Some historians say her name should be spelled like bird woman sounds in Hidatsa—*Sakakawea*.

The Shoshone spell the name *Sacajawea* with a *j*, but they disagree on its meaning. One of the early claims was that *Sacajawea* was a Shoshone word for "boat launcher" or "boat puller." Because the Shoshones often named someone for a characteristic event or quality, it is possible that the tribe could have given her that name when she returned to them accompanied by men who were pulling canoes up a shallow river. More recently, some Shoshone speakers have said that *Sacajawea* means "burden" or "one who bears a burden." Still other Shoshone language authorities say that it is not a recognizable Shoshone name.

Most historians prefer *Sacagawea*, primarily because that spelling is closest to the way the name appears in the original journals. But the questions of how to spell the name and its true meaning remain a sensitive issue among historians and the people of the Shoshone and Hidatsa tribes.

these journals were men from a very different culture and none of them spoke Sacagawea's language.

Beginning in the late 1800s, writers and novelists who told the story of Sacagawea often added their own fictional details to journal accounts or invented new tales about her. One of these authors was Eva Emery Dye, who in 1902 published a novel in which she inaccurately portrayed the Shoshone woman as a princess. However, she also characterized Sacagawea as a strong, self-reliant, and capable woman who had made great contributions to the historic expedition in which she traveled. The journal writings made during the Lewis and Clark Expedition support this portrait as that of the real Sacagawea—a woman who contributed in many ways to an expedition that helped shape American history.

2

A SHOSHONE GIRL

Because the Shoshone had no written language, much of their past has been lost or forgotten. Oral traditions—stories passed on by tribal elders—tell more about Shoshone culture and religious beliefs than about the tribe's history.

LAND OF THE SHOSHONE

Historians believe that as many as two to three thousand years ago, the Shoshone migrated north from the Great Basin—a region encompassing most of today's Nevada and western Utah. Various tribes eventually settled over a vast region east and west of the Rocky Mountains.

As one Shoshone group passed through the mountains of present-day Idaho, they came to a river that teemed with salmon. The people decided to settle in the stream's long, narrow valley, naming it *Pah-dai*, which is Shoshone for "our water." Today, this area is known as the Lemhi River Valley. The members of this Eastern Shoshone tribe,

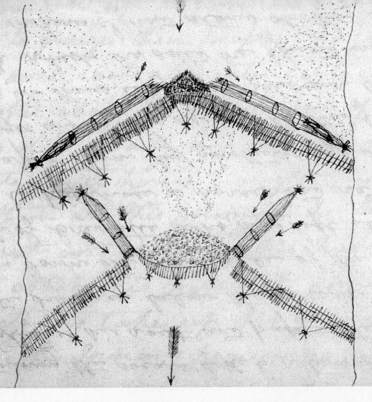

A Shoshone fishing weir. Sacagawea's people fished salmon with spears, basketry traps, and weirs—stick enclosures set in streams to capture fish. During the early spring and late summer months millions of salmon would swim upstream from the Pacific Ocean, sometimes traveling distances of more than 800 miles (1,288 kilometers) in order to spawn and die in the streams and rivers where they had been born.

also known as the Agaidika, or salmon-eaters, were Sacagawea's ancestors.

The Shoshone centered their lives upon the annual return of the salmon, but also hunted wild game (mostly small animals such as rabbits) and gathered plants for food and medicine. They were a nomadic people, traveling from one temporary camp to another according to the season when the fish, game, or plants would be available in the greatest quantities.

THE SHOSHONE WAY OF LIFE

Members of the tribe divided their labor according to gender. Men hunted and fished. They defended the tribe when it was attacked, and they raided enemy tribes. Shoshone women did most of the work within the camp. They butchered animals the men had killed, tanned the hides, and sewed them to make new clothing or bedding. They supplemented the meat diet by gathering roots, berries, seeds, and nuts. The Shoshone women prepared meals, made baskets and pottery, and dried food so that it could be stored and used during the winter. When Sacagawea was growing up, she learned these skills from her mother and other women of the village.

One of the most important events in Shoshone history happened around 80 years before Sacagawea was born. Sometime in the early 1700s members of the tribe acquired horses, most likely from other Native American

By the early 1800s, the Lemhi Shoshone owned around 700 Spanish mustangs, like the ones shown here. Many of the horses and the equipment used to ride them were obtained through trading at Spanish settlements to the south.

tribes to the south such as the Ute and Comanche, who traded with the Spanish. With these Spanish mustangs, or barbs, the Shoshone could travel farther and faster, carrying more belongings and greater quantities of food. The horse also enabled the Shoshone to hunt larger animals, such as antelope, deer, elk, and buffalo.

BUFFALO HUNTERS

As the number of Shoshone men with horses grew, the tribe began migrating each year to the central plains of present-day Montana to hunt buffalo. Tribes that hunted buffalo lived very well. Just about every part of a buffalo carcass—from the meat to the skin to the bones—could be put to use as food, clothing, or tools. The Shoshone cut the meat into thin strips that they dried in the sun and wind. This jerky gave them a new source of food for the long winters in their homeland. The women tanned the buffalo hides and sewed them into large tepees weighing as much as several hundred pounds. Only a horse could manage such a burden.

The horse allowed the Shoshone to obtain a greater food supply than was possible when hunting on foot. However, tracking buffalo by horseback on the plains also exposed the Shoshone to danger. The central plains of present-day Mondtana were a hunting ground used by many other Native American tribes, and when two tribes met there, they sometimes fought. Wars began that lasted for generations, with weaker tribes forced to migrate to new areas.

The Shoshone were the first tribe in the region to acquire horses, and they were relatively unchallenged in their hunting grounds for several decades. But gradually, the tribe's enemies acquired their own horses. And at some point in the mid-1700s, firearms introduced by

European Americans tilted the balance of power against the Shoshone. Muskets proved to be more effective weapons than the Shoshone's arrows or war clubs, and without firearms of their own the Shoshone could not stand and fight on equal terms. The tribe traded with the Spanish living to the south, but they refused to supply the Indians with guns.

Because the Shoshone had come to depend upon dried buffalo meat as a winter food source, they continued to conduct their annual hunt, but they took precautions. Sometimes the men would take extra horses with them so that they could escape quickly if attacked. Or hunters would travel with their allies, such as the Montana Salish, so they could provide more protection.

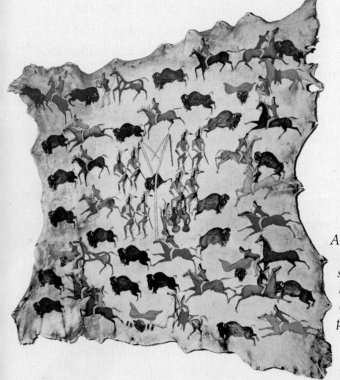

A 19th-century Shoshone buffalo hunt painted on elk skin. The ability to hunt buffalo from horseback ensured an abundant supply of food and clothing for the Shoshone, who also used the skins to build portable shelters, or tepees.

And, sometimes, only small bands of Shoshone would set out in order to hunt quickly, retreating back to the mountains before their better-armed enemies could discover them.

By the early 1800s the Shoshone had been pushed into the mountains by hostile Plains tribes such as the Blackfeet and Hidatsa. These tribes had been able to obtain muskets from the French traders in the north.

CAPTURED BY THE HIDATSA

One buffalo hunt around the year 1800 changed Sacagawea's life. She was probably 12 years old—old enough to have been promised in marriage to a Shoshone man twice her age, but not old enough yet to have become his wife. Modern historians know the story only because Sacagawea shared it with her companions in the Corps of Discovery when the party reached the place where the attack had occurred.

Sacagawea explained that the Shoshone were camped at the Three Forks of the Missouri—a place where three tributaries of the Missouri River come together, in present-day western Montana. Suddenly, the Hidatsa attacked. In the July 28, 1805, journal entry written by Lewis, he recorded the story of Sacagawea's capture,

The Nez Perce from the northwest and the Flathead Indians from the Bitterroot Valley to the north often came to the Lemhi Valley to fish and trade with the Shoshone. It is also believed that the three tribes may have united, from time to time, to hunt buffalo together and give themselves more protection against hostile Plains tribes.

referring to the Shoshone as the "Snake Indians" and to the far western tributary as "Jeffersons river":

> Our present camp is precisely on the spot that the Snake Indians were encamped at the time the [Hidatsa] of the Knife R[iver] first came in sight of them five years since. from hence they retreated about three miles up Jeffersons river and concealed themselves in the woods, the [Hidatsa] pursued, attacked them, killed 4 men 4 women a number of boys, and mad[e] prisoners of all the females and four boys, *Sah-cah-gar-we-ah* [our] Indian woman was one of the female prisoners taken at that time.

Lewis doesn't say this in his journal, but Sacagawea's parents were likely among those killed by the Hidatsa. One of Sacagawea's friends was taken prisoner but managed to escape and return safely home. The Hidatsa took Sacagawea and the other prisoners to their villages on the Knife and Missouri Rivers, in present-day North Dakota.

THE KNIFE RIVER PEOPLE

No account of Sacagawea's life as a captive has ever been discovered, so no one knows what she did with the Hidatsa or how her captors treated her. She was probably assimilated into the Hidatsa community, which was very different from the society she had left.

Other nomadic tribes of the Plains were the Sioux and Blackfeet. Enemies of the Shoshone, they hunted on foot or on horseback and lived in tepees made from buffalo skins.

This 1832 oil painting by George Catlin shows the earth-covered lodges of a Hidatsa village on the Knife River as they would have looked in 1810. Each earth lodge housed up to 20 people, and also included enough room for the best hunting horses and warhorses.

Sacagawea had been stolen from one of the poorest and most isolated tribes in North America and taken to live in one of the wealthiest, largest Indian communities on the continent. Unlike the nomadic Shoshone, who lived in simple tepees, the Hidatsa people lived in permanent villages, in earth lodges capable of housing several families and even horses during the long winters on the northern plains.

The Hidatsa lived in three villages along the Knife River. They were allied with the Mandan, who lived in two villages a few miles away on the Missouri River. In the early 1800s, the Knife River villages made up one of the largest Native American communities on the continent. Several thousand people populated the five Hidatsa and Mandan villages, more than lived in St. Louis or Washington, D.C., at that time.

Like the Shoshone, Hidatsa men hunted bison and other game, and Hidatsa women gathered wild plants for food. However, the Hidatsa women also grew vegetables such as corn, squash, pumpkins, and beans in large gardens. They dried and stored their crops in pits within the earth lodges. If the harvest was good, they traded the surplus to other tribes for things they needed. In Hidatsa society, the women owned their gardens as well as the earth lodges in which they lived.

The Knife River villages were centers for robust trade among Native American tribes. And the Hidatsa and Mandan also traded with the French Canadians, who exchanged European muskets and manufactured goods for valuable furs and hides.

THE FUR TRADE

The North American fur trade had begun in the 16th century when French sailors traveled to the coast of Newfoundland to fish. They would barter with the Native Americans they met, offering small goods like metal knives, beads, mirrors, and other items in exchange for fur pelts.

In the early 1600s, as demand for beaver pelts exploded in Europe, French colonial leaders like Samuel de Champlain expanded the fur trade in North America. Between 1669 and 1683, the French explorer René-Robert Cavelier, Sieur de La Salle, explored the Mississippi River, claiming the entire region drained by the mighty waterway for France. La Salle named this vast region La Louisiane after the French King Louis XIV.

By the early 1700s, the French had established a network of forts and trading outposts along the Mississippi

River and throughout the Great Lakes region. Major settlements were established at St. Louis and New Orleans. In the unsettled areas, French traders lived among the natives, trading guns, blankets, alcohol, and metal tools for Indian trappers' bales of beaver pelts.

Many French traders traveled west from the Mississippi by way of the Missouri River, a water route used by both Indian and Euro-American trappers and traders. Located along the Missouri and Knife Rivers, the Mandan and Hidatsa Indian villages soon became the center of a trading network that stretched from the Great Lakes to the northern Rocky Mountains.

A trap hangs from the post and drying frame holding a beaver pelt. During the early 1800s beaver fur was a valuable commodity in the United States, and the Mandan and Hidatsa villages served as a major center for the fur trade.

TOUSSAINT CHARBONNEAU

One of the French-Canadian traders living with the Hidatsa was Toussaint Charbonneau. He had been born near Montreal, Canada, probably in 1767. As a young man he entered the fur trade, working first for the Montreal-based Northwest Company and then independently. Around 1797 Charbonneau settled at Knife River, where in his dealings with the Hidatsa he gained a basic understanding of their language. Sometime in the early 1800s he took Sacagawea as his wife.

Charbonneau is believed to have married Sacagawea according to the Hidatsa custom, which was similar to the Shoshone custom. A man who wanted to take a woman as his wife offered gifts to the male who was responsible for her: a father, brother, uncle, or other relative. The arrangement happened some time before the spring of 1804, because by then Sacagawea was pregnant. Charbonneau had one other wife, who was also Shoshone. He lived with them in the Hidatsa village called Metaharta.

Living in the wilderness with the Hidatsa, Sacagawea and Charbonneau had no way of knowing about the plans to explore the west being made by the new leader of the United States of America, President Thomas Jefferson. The young Shoshone woman would never meet the man who was about to launch the expedition that would make her one of the most famous women in American history.

THE LEWIS AND CLARK EXPEDITION

President Thomas Jefferson had long wished to see the land west of the Mississippi River explored and documented scientifically. The "West" fascinated him. When he was elected president of the United States in 1800, he finally had his opportunity.

Jefferson selected Meriwether Lewis, a former army officer and Jefferson's private secretary, to lead the expedition. To prepare for the mission, Lewis moved into the White House, where he had access to Jefferson's extensive library of books and papers on the natural sciences. He also traveled to Lancaster and Philadelphia, in Pennsylvania, where President Jefferson's scientific colleagues instructed him in the latest studies in botany, biology, astronomical navigation, and medicine.

SEEKING A PASSAGE TO THE PACIFIC

Jefferson needed reasons other than scientific curiosity to send an expedition to the West. There would be economic advantages from funding such a journey, he explained to

The third president of the United States, serving from 1801 to 1809, Thomas Jefferson believed that exploration of the West could serve several purposes: find a river passageway to the Pacific, establish the U.S. government's authority in the region, and allow for a scientific survey of the native animals and plants. (Opposite) A copy of Jefferson's confidential letter to the Senate and House of Representatives requesting funding in January 1803 for an expedition to the West. At the time, the U.S. government had no official claim to the Louisiana Territory or legal right to explore the region.

Congress in January 1803, when he asked U.S. legislators to cover the project's expenses. An expedition to the West, Jefferson argued, would establish the basis for extending American trade into new regions.

To this end, Jefferson's chief goal for the Lewis and Clark Expedition was the discovery of a transportation route across North America, preferably a water route that boats could use. For years, explorers had sought a Northwest Passage, a water route from the Atlantic to Pacific Oceans. Many people were convinced that such a waterway existed, but, as of the early 1800s, the Missouri River had only been mapped as far upstream as present-day North Dakota. In the far west, explorers from ships traveling along the Pacific coast had ventured up the Columbia River as far as present-day Portland, Oregon.

Jefferson hoped a Northwest Passage existed within the unknown lands that lay in between the Missouri River and Columbia River systems. And he wanted his expedition to

Confidential.

Gentlemen of the Senate and of the House of Representatives.

As the continuance of the Act for establishing trading houses with the Indian tribes will be under the consideration of the legislature at it's present session, I think it my duty to communicate the views which have guided me in the execution of that act; in order that you may decide on the policy of continuing it, in the present or any other form, or to discontinue it altogether if that shall, on the whole, seem most for the public good.

The Indian tribes residing within the limits of the US. have for a considerable time been growing more & more uneasy at the constant diminution of the territory they occupy, altho' effected by their own voluntary sales: and the policy has long been gaining strength with them of refusing absolutely, all further sale on any conditions. insomuch that, at this time, it hazards their friendship, and excites dangerous jealousies & perturbations in their minds to make any overture for the purchase of the smallest portions of their land. a very few tribes only are not yet obstinately in these dispositions. In order peaceably to counteract this policy of theirs, and to provide an extension of territory which the rapid increase of our numbers will call for, two measures are deemed expedient. First, to encourage them to abandon hunting, to apply to the raising stock, to agriculture and domestic manufactures, and thereby prove to themselves that less land & labour will maintain them in this, better than in their former mode of living. the extensive forests necessary in the hunting life, will then become useless, & they will see advantage in exchanging them for the means of improving their farms, & of increasing their domestic comforts. Secondly to multiply trading houses among them, & place within their reach those things which will contribute more to their domestic comfort than the possession of extensive, but uncultivated wilds. experience & reflection will develope to them the wisdom of exchanging what they can spare & we want, for what we can spare and they want. in leading them thus to agriculture, to

[fragment overlay]

our ...
... plo...
traver...
within ...
... ally adm...
the natio...
in the hab...

... regarding this as a literary pursuit which it is
... permitting within it's dominions, would not be disposed to view it
with jealousy. even if the expiring state of it's interests there did not render it a
matter of indifference. The appropriation of two thousand five hundred dollars
for the purpose of extending the external commerce of the US. while understood and
considered by the Executive as giving the legislative sanction, would cover the undertaking from notice, and prevent the obstructions which interested individuals
might otherwise previously prepare in it's way.

... an additional gratification.
... it should incident.

Jan. 18. 1803.

31

find it. In his instructions to Lewis, written in 1803, Jefferson stated:

> The object of your mission is to explore the Missouri river, & such principal stream of it, as, by [its] course and communication with the waters of the Pacific ocean . . . may offer the most direct & practicable water communication across this continent for the purposes of commerce.

The lucrative fur trade was of particular interest to Jefferson, who wanted U.S. traders to gain a foothold in business dominated at the time by the French.

THE LOUISIANA PURCHASE

When Jefferson took office, the western boundary of the United States was the Mississippi River. West of the Mississippi lay a vast region claimed by France. Known as the Louisiana Territory, it reached from the Gulf Coast westward to the mountains that form the border of what is now Idaho and Montana. To the north, the Louisiana Territory included the Missouri River watershed— an immense area containing the creeks, streams, and smaller rivers that drained into the Missouri.

Captain Meriwether Lewis was chosen to head the expedition to explore the West, as Jefferson explained in a letter to his friend Benjamin Smith Barton, because Lewis exhibited the "character, prudence, habits adopted to the woods, & a familiarity with the Indian manners & character, requisite for this undertaking."

In 1803, Jefferson learned that the French emperor, Napoleon, was willing to sell the land to the United States. Although Jefferson was unsure if the U.S. Constitution allowed him to make the purchase, he finally decided that it was best for the future of his country. With the Louisiana Purchase Treaty, signed in April 1803 and ratified by Congress the following October, Jefferson doubled the size of the United States and greatly increased the importance of the planned expedition.

When invited by Lewis to join the expedition to the West, William Clark responded with enthusiasm, writing: "My friend I assure you no man lives with whome I would perfur to undertake Such a Trip &c as your self."

Lewis, and Clark would go as official representatives of the United States to all the tribes they would meet along the way. Jefferson instructed Lewis to tell the Indian nations that he wished them to live in peace with each other and with the United States.

THE EXPEDITION GETS UNDER WAY

On June 19, 1803, Lewis wrote to his friend and former army commander William Clark to offer him co-command of the Corps of Discovery. After Clark eagerly accepted, Lewis asked him to recruit some good hunters and woodsmen for the expedition.

Lewis spent the summer of 1803 purchasing supplies and equipment. He arranged to have it freighted in wagons to Pittsburgh, Pennsylvania, where he had a specially designed keelboat constructed. At the end of August he set off down

Consisting of 828,000 square miles (2,144,520 square km), the vast region known as the Louisiana Territory was purchased by the United States for $15,000,000, plus interest, or about $28.04 per square mile. Congress ratified the Louisiana Purchase Treaty in October 1803.

the Ohio River with 11 men to join William Clark, who was headquartered in Louisville, in the new state of Kentucky.

After meeting up with Clark, Lewis and the rest of his men headed to St. Louis and the confluence of the Missouri and Mississippi Rivers. As they made their way down the Ohio River and up the Mississippi, the captains recruited volunteers. That winter, the approximately 40 members of the expedition made final preparations at a fort they had built and named Camp River Dubois, located at the mouth of the Missouri River, just upstream from St. Louis.

The following spring, in May 1804, the expedition set out up the Missouri River aboard the keelboat and two rowboat-like boats, known as pirogues (one painted red, and the other, white). The men of the Corps were traveling against the current, against a river that challenged them with hidden obstacles, sandbars, riffles, and eddies. The weather was extremely hot, and was often accompanied by furious thunderstorms and strong winds. Ticks and mosquitoes, Clark noted in his journal "are verry troublesome."

Averaging about 10 miles per day, the Corps soon reached the vast North American grasslands known as the Great Plains. There, they sighted wildlife that was new and strange to them—prairie dogs, coyotes, mule deer,

*(Right) William Clark's field notes show the 55-foot long and 8-foot wide shallow-hulled boat used at the beginning of the expedition. Named Discovery, the vessel could carry about 10 tons of cargo and be moved upstream by being sailed, poled like a raft, or towed from the riverbank.
(Above) Reconstruction of the Discovery keelboat with reenactors in military garb that expedition members would have worn.*

antelopes, and jackrabbits. The men were astounded by the immense size of buffalo herds, which numbered in the thousands.

AMBASSADORS FOR JEFFERSON

As they traveled, Lewis and Clark held peaceful councils with various Indian tribes. The first formal meeting between representatives of the United States and western Indians took place on August 3, when the Otos and Missouris came to a meeting held near what is now Council Bluffs, Iowa. During the council, the soldiers marched in uniform and demonstrated their weapons, showing the military strength of the U.S. government.

The expedition would follow this kind of protocol for subsequent Indian councils. Typically, Lewis and Clark would give the leaders peace medals, along with American flags and various gifts. They would show off the advanced technology the expedition carried, such as magnets, compasses, telescopes, and an air gun. And they would inform the tribal leaders that the U.S. president was their new "great father," who wanted them to live in peace with each other and with whites. In exchange, the Indian leaders were told, they would gain access to additional trade and military protection.

In late September, the expedition encountered the Teton Sioux, who regarded themselves as masters of the Missouri. The Sioux controlled traffic passing on the river and

A mong the new recruits for the expedition were men of Native American ancestry. George Drouillard, Pierre Cruzatte, and François Labiche were sons of French-Canadian fathers and Indian mothers.

demanded the expedition pay a toll of tobacco. After an aggressive standoff, including a show of arms, the Corps of Discovery avoided a fight with the Teton Sioux and continued on up the river.

On October 8, the members of the expedition reached and held a council with the Arikara, who lived at the mouth of the Grand River, in present-day northern South Dakota. Like the Mandans and Hidatsa, the Arikara lived in round, covered earth lodges, but this encounter was the first time Lewis and Clark's men had ever seen this type of Indian shelter.

(Above) Captains Lewis and Clark holding a council with the Indians, as depicted in the journal of Patrick Gass. (Right) To demonstrate the authority of the U.S. government, Lewis and Clark would present a placard containing a message from President Thomas Jefferson and hand out peace medals that showed the president on one side and hands clasped in a handshake on the other.

FROM ST. LOUIS TO THE KNIFE RIVER VILLAGES

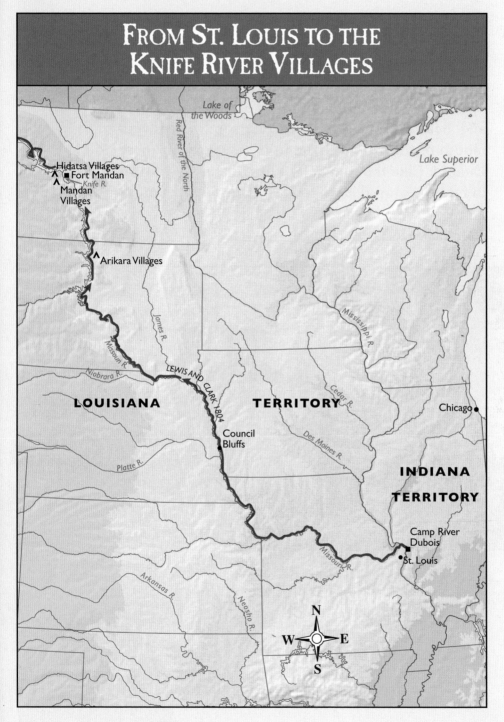

To display the wealth of the United States, Lewis and Clark distributed gifts to the Indian tribes they encountered. As the following list from the expedition manifest shows, presents included pipe tomahawks, handkerchiefs, ivory combs, and knives.

THE MANDAN AND HIDATSA

In late October, the arrival of the Corps of Discovery caused great excitement among the Mandan and Hidatsa. Up until that time, only two parties from St. Louis had ever reached Knife River, primarily because of the presence of the powerful Teton Sioux on the Missouri.

Lewis and Clark invited the Mandan and Hidatsa chiefs to a council. In the October 29, 1804, entry in his journal, Sergeant Patrick Gass described how the Americans established authority with the Mandan and Hidatsa:

Jefferson's Instructions to Lewis

President Jefferson wanted detailed information about the Indian tribes the expedition would meet. In a letter to Lewis, Jefferson wrote:

> You will . . . endeavor to make yourself acquainted
> . . . with the names of the nations & their numbers;
>
> the extent & limits of their possessions;
>
> their relations with other tribes of nations;
>
> their language, traditions, monuments;
>
> their ordinary occupations in agriculture, fishing, hunting, war, arts, & the implements for these;
>
> their food, clothing, & domestic accommodations;
>
> the diseases prevalent among them, & the remedies they use;
>
> moral & physical circumstances which distinguish them from the tribes we know;
>
> peculiarities in their laws, customs, & dispositions;
>
> and articles of commerce they may need or furnish, & to what extent.

[A] shot was fired from our bow piece, and the commanding officers took the chiefs by the hand. Captain Lewis, through an interpreter, delivered a speech; gave a suit of clothes to each of the chiefs and some articles for their villages.

The water level in the Missouri river was dropping, which made traveling up the river more difficult. Rather than continue on, the Americans decided to spend the winter among the friendly Mandan and Hidatsa.

THE SHOSHONE "INTERPRETRESS"

Meriwether Lewis and William Clark realized that spending the winter with the Mandan and Hidatsa Indians could provide the opportunity for them to learn a great deal of information about the land, rivers, and people to the west. The Hidatsa were familiar with the country near the headwaters of the Missouri because their war parties regularly raided the Shoshone people who lived there.

The Corps of Discovery chose a spot downstream and across the river from the main Mandan village to build a camp. Here, the members of the expedition would spend the winter of 1804–05.

A JOB WITH THE CORPS

Toussaint Charbonneau was away on a hunting trip when the Lewis and Clark Expedition arrived at the Knife River villages. Upon his return, he recognized an opportunity to get a job and went down the river to see the Americans.

Charbonneau found members of the Corps falling trees and erecting log cabins. Most were soldiers, but there were also several French-speaking boatmen, who had been hired to help row and pull the keelboat and pirogues up the Missouri River. Because he spoke little or no English, Charbonneau may have asked one of these

A Mandan village, painted by George Catlin in 1832. Captains Lewis and Clark decided to set up winter camp close to the Mandan and Hidatsa villages so they would have the opportunity to question the Indians, who were knowledgeable about the upper reaches of the Missouri River and lands to the west.

men to introduce him to the two officers who were supervising the work. Captain William Clark wrote in his journal on November 4 that

> a Mr. Chaubonée, interpeter for the [Hidatsa] nation Came to See us . . . this man wished to hire as an interpeter.

Charbonneau was right. Meriwether Lewis and William Clark could use someone to translate the Hidatsa language. They had already hired René Jessaume, another Frenchman, to interpret Mandan. The Mandan would be their closest neighbors that winter, but the Hidatsa had more knowledge about the upper Missouri River.

Charbonneau told Lewis and Clark that one of his two Shoshone women—Sacagawea—was a member of the tribe that lived at the headwaters of the Missouri. The Shoshones owned horses, which Lewis and Clark realized could be useful to the expedition when it had to cross the Continental Divide—the mountainous area separating the headwaters of the Missouri and Columbia Rivers.

Lewis and Clark asked Charbonneau if he and his woman would come with them when they traveled up the Missouri River in the spring of 1805. Charbonneau accepted the offer.

First Meeting

After his interview, Charbonneau returned home to tell Sacagawea that the American explorers had hired him to interpret Hidatsa and her to interpret Shoshone. During the four years since her kidnapping, Sacagawea's only contacts with her Shoshone past were other Shoshone captives. She now had the opportunity to find her people again.

43

In his diary, Sergeant John Ordway described Sacagawea's first meeting with the Corps of Discovery. It was November 11, 1804, he wrote, and the men were filling the chinks between the logs of their cabins with mud:

> [A] clear and pleasant morning. we commenced dobbing our huts & covering them &.C. a frenchman's Squaw came to our camp who belonged to the [Shoshone] nation She came with our Intreperters wife & brought with them 4 buffalow Robes and Gave them to our officers.

Although several men in the expedition kept journals, no one ever described what Sacagawea looked like in any detail. Clark wrote that her skin was lighter colored than Charbonneau's other Shoshone wife, and that both women were remarkably small. Since the average height for women at that time was about five feet three inches, they were probably well under five feet tall.

FORT MANDAN

Sacagawea was six months pregnant when she, Charbonneau and his other Shoshone wife moved into Fort Mandan, named by Lewis and Clark in honor of their Indian neighbors. Charbonneau and his two wives shared a small cabin with the Mandan interpreter René Jessaume, his wife, and their daughter and son.

The expedition captains wanted both Charbonneau and Jessaume to live at Fort Mandan. That way, Lewis and Clark could learn a great deal about the Mandan and Hidatsa people, as well as find out what they knew about other tribes and the geography of the surrounding region.

However, obtaining information took a great deal of time and patience. Communication needed to pass through several interpreters and languages. For example, if Clark wanted to ask Sacagawea a question about the Shoshones, he would first put the question in English to someone who spoke both English and French, usually Private François Labiche. Labiche would then ask the same question in French to Toussaint Charbonneau, who spoke French and Hidatsa. He would then speak to his wife in Hidatsa, the language they spoke with each other. To answer the question, the translators repeated the process in reverse.

BIRTH OF A SON

On February 11, Lewis reported in his journal that "about five oclock this evening one of the wives of Charbono was

Named for the nearby Indian tribe, Fort Mandan became Sacagawea's home in November 1804, when her husband signed on with the Lewis and Clark Expedition. This full-scale reconstruction of Fort Mandan at Washburn, North Dakota, is located on the north side of the Missouri River, a few miles downstream from the actual site.

delivered of a fine boy." Because Sacagawea was young, small, and having her first baby, her labor had been "tedious and the pain violent," wrote Lewis.

The young woman struggled to give birth, assisted by the Mandan interpreter, Jessaume. He told Lewis that it was possible to speed the birth of a child by administering a "small portion of the rattle of the rattle-snake." Lewis had rattlesnake rattles with his medicines, and he provided two rings that Jessaume crushed and put in a small amount of water for Sacagawea to drink. Lewis was later told that within ten minutes of drinking the potion, she gave birth to her son. However, in his journal he questioned whether the rattlesnake rattle had actually hastened the delivery, writing, "I must confess that I want faith as to it's efficacy."

The son of Sacagawea and Charbonneau was named Jean Baptiste. He would later receive the nickname of

Lewis didn't need interpreters to collect some of the information that Jefferson wanted about the Indian tribes. The expedition captain's own observations, for example, were sufficient to describe the homes, clothing, tools, food, and weapons of the various groups he encountered. But he needed skilled interpreters and a great deal of time and patience to obtain other information that Jefferson requested, such as their traditions, laws, and customs.

Sacagawea could help Lewis learn about the Shoshones by sharing her memories and, if they could find her people, by putting Lewis's questions to the Shoshones he met. In addition, if the Corps of Discovery found Shoshones living among other tribes, Sacagawea could be called upon to interpret through them. Her assistance in gathering information on Indian nations would be one of her most important contributions to the expedition.

This 1912 painting by Edgar S. Paxson shows members of the expedition, from left to right: John Colter, York, Meriwether Lewis, William Clark, Sacagawea, and Toussaint Charbonneau.

Pompy or Pomp. Some historians believe the name Pompy is Shoshone, meaning either leader or head. Other sources say the name Pompy or Little Pomp was later given to the child by Clark as a sign of his growing affection for the child.

PREPARATIONS FOR THE JOURNEY

Soon after Pompy's birth, the Corps of Discovery prepared to resume their voyage up the Missouri River. Having determined that the large keelboat was too big to navigate the shallow waters they would encounter on the upper Missouri, Lewis and Clark made plans to send the boat back to St. Louis. A small crew of soldiers was assigned the task of getting the keelboat safely down the river. They would carry letters and reports to President

47

Jefferson as well as some of the collected items, including plant and animal specimens and Indian artifacts.

To replace the keelboat, Lewis and Clark had the men construct six dugout canoes, each about 30 feet long and about 3 feet wide, from the trunks of cottonwood trees. By the end of March, the new boats were ready.

During that time, Charbonneau made a mistake that almost cost him his job with the Corps. He issued several demands to Lewis and Clark, including the privilege of not having to do guard duty. This was a nighttime assignment requiring him to take turns with the soldiers in protecting the camp.

The captains told Charbonneau they could not agree to his demands and asked him to reconsider. The next

An example of the crude dugout canoes that were built by the Corps of Discovery.

day Charbonneau stated that he had not changed his mind, so Lewis and Clark expressed their regrets and told the Hidatsa interpreter they would find someone to replace him. Charbonneau packed up his baggage and family and left the fort. However, several days later, he sent word to Lewis and Clark that he would agree to the original terms after all. Lewis and Clark suspected that Canadian fur traders, hoping to cause problems for the U.S. expedition, had encouraged Charbonneau to make his demands.

LEAVING THE KNIFE RIVER VILLAGES

On April 7, both detachments of the Corps pushed their boats into the Missouri River and set off. The keelboat drifted downstream, on its way to St. Louis. From there, the materials that Lewis and Clark had collected would be shipped to President Jefferson, who would receive them the following August. Among the plant specimens were Indian corn, sagebrush, and cottonwood. Of the five live animals shipped—a prairie dog and four magpies—only the prairie dog and one of the birds would survive.

The 33 members of the "permanent party," headed upstream. In his journal entry that day, Clark listed the names of the members of the permanent party, which included Lewis and Clark, 3 sergeants, 23 privates, the slave York, French-Canadian interpreter Drouillard, as well as:

> Shabonah [Charbonneau] and his *Indian Squar* to
> act as an Interpreter & interpretress for the snake
> Indians...& Shabonahs infant. *Sah-kah-gar we a*

This written record was the first time that Sacagawea's name appeared in a journal entry.

Sacagawea's son, Jean Baptiste Charbonneau, was about two months old when the Corps of Discovery explorers left Fort Mandan on April 7, 1805, bound for the Pacific Ocean. Sacagawea would carry her child as he grew from infant to toddler during the 16 months that they spent traveling with the Lewis and Clark Expedition.

Most members of the expedition were heading into the unknown, to lands that had never been seen or mapped by white people. However, the journey was taking one person with the expedition closer to her home with each day's travel.

Seeking the Headwaters of the Missouri

The men in the Corps of Discovery recognized that Sacagawea would be great help once they reached the lands of the Shoshone. The day after the expedition left Fort Mandan, on April 8, Sergeant Patrick Gass recorded in his journal:

> The woman that is with us is a squaw of the Snake nation of Indians, and wife to our interpreter. We expect she will be of service to us, when passing through that nation.

More Than Just an Interpreter

However, it soon became apparent that Sacagawea would be useful to the Corps in more ways than as a Shoshone interpreter. While living among both the Shoshone and

Hidatsa, she had learned much about medicinal and food plants. From the start, she used these skills to add to provisions for the Corps. On April 9, for example, Lewis wrote:

> [W]hen we halted for dinner the squaw busied herself in serching for the wild artichokes which the mice collect and deposit in large hoards. this operation she performed by penetrating the earth with a sharp stick about some small collections of drift wood. her labour soon proved successful, and she procurrd a good quantity of these roots.

The roots and berries Sacagawea gathered during the expedition added variety to the normal diet of meat obtained by hunting buffalo and other game.

As the canoes of the Corps of Discovery traveled up the waters of the Missouri River, they could be easily spotted by local Indians. This 1896 painting by Charles M. Russell, entitled "Indians Discovering Lewis and Clark," depicts their probable reaction.

As the men came across plants and animals they hadn't seen before, Sacagawea explained how her people used them and where they came from. For example, on April 29, when the explorers saw their first bighorn sheep, she explained that the animals were very common in the Rocky Mountains. A day later, after finding a species of currant that was native to her mountain homelands, she brought Clark the small shrub, explaining that it "bore a delicious froot and that great quantites" grew in the mountains.

FRIENDSHIP WITH CLARK

By day, the members of the Corps made their way up the Missouri River, traveling by foot and by water. Some rode in the boats, while others hunted or explored the surrounding countryside. When game animals were plentiful and hunting went well, the explorers would eat as much as ten pounds of meat per person a day.

In order to see more of the area, as well as collect specimens, either Clark or Lewis would typically walk along the river shoreline, while the other stayed with the boats. Whenever Clark traveled on foot along the shoreline, Charbonneau and Sacagawea often accompanied him. A friendship between Clark and the Charbonneau family soon developed—one that would last for many years.

A NEAR ACCIDENT

All the boats had sails that were used when the wind was right and the river current not too strong. Rowing and paddling upstream was hard work, so the opportunity to let the wind take over was welcomed.

Because Lewis and Clark believed that the safest boat they had was the white pirogue, they put the most important

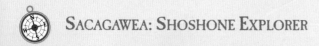

Traveling against the current up the Missouri River was slow and difficult. Tree branches and roots jutting into the water hampered progress and capsized canoes, as this image from the published journal of Patrick Gass shows.

cargo on it: scientific instruments, medicines, books and journals, and gifts for Indians, "in short," wrote Lewis, "almost every article indispensibly necessary to . . . insure the success of the [expedition]." For the same reason, the three men who could not swim (which included Touissant Charbonneau), as well as Sacagawea and her infant, were aboard the white boat.

The pirogue was steered with a tiller in the stern, or rear, of the boat. Less than a week after the expedition had set off, Captain Meriwether Lewis described in his journal entry of April 13 how the group avoided a potentially serious accident:

> [W]e therefore hoisted both the sails in the White Perogue . . . which carried her at a pretty good gate, untill about 2 in the afternoon when a suddon squall of wind struck us.

Charbonneau was at the tiller of the white pirogue when a sudden wind gust tilted the boat to one side. He panicked and turned the tiller so that the boat was sideways to the wind. Fortunately, the wind dropped before the boat capsized, and George Drouillard took Charbonneau's place at the tiller. If the boat had tipped over and spilled its passengers and cargo into the river, Lewis wrote, "[T]his accedent was very near costing us dearly." The passengers aboard the boat, he added, "would most probably have perished, as the waves were high, and the pirogue upwards of 200 yards from the nearest shore."

A WOMAN OF "EQUAL FORTITUDE"

A month later, with Charbonneau again at the tiller, the white pirogue came close to capsizing once more. This time the boat turned over so far that water poured in over the side. Charbonneau froze with terror. One of the crewmembers, Pierre Cruzatte, shouted and pointed his gun at Charbonneau, threatening to shoot him if he didn't attend to the tiller. Meanwhile, Sacagawea remained calm, retrieving the papers, books, instruments, and other important items from the water before they floated away.

Finally, Charbonneau returned to his senses, and managed to right the boat. Afterward, the party had to land to dry out the wet cargo. In his journal entry written two days later, Lewis remarked on Sacagawea's courage during the incident:

> The Indian woman to whom I ascribe equal fortitude and resolution, with any person onboard at the time of the accedent, caught and preserved most of the light articles which were washed overboard.

55

The following week, on May 20, Lewis and Clark named a river for Sacawagea to honor her courage. That day Lewis wrote in his journal:

> [A]bout five miles above the mouth of shell river a handsome river of about fifty yards in width discharged itself into the shell river . . . this stream we called *Sah ca gah we a* or bird woman's River, after our interpreter the Snake woman.

The Sacagawea River is a tributary of the Musselshell River, which joins the Missouri River in present-day central Montana.

A DANGEROUS ILLNESS

In early June, the group encountered a fork in the river. Lewis and Clark were uncertain about which route to

This journal page from May 20, 1805, notes the decision to name a river after Sacagawea.

take. After scouting the region, they determined that the wide, rapid-moving westward river was the Missouri—the river they needed to follow. Lewis named the other water-way Maria's River, in honor of his cousin, or the Marias.

At the mouth of the Marias, the men buried supplies intended for later use. To create this storage area, or cache, they dug a hole about six or seven feet deep, and laid the floor with a layer of dry sticks before placing the provisions and equipment inside.

The Corps continued up the Missouri and in mid-June came upon a massive set of falls, known as the Great Falls. To continue their journey, the captains realized, the group would have to leave the other pirogue behind and carry the canoes. Lewis left the group in order to scout out the best portage path. The remaining members of the expedition remained at the falls, and buried the equipment they didn't need in another cache.

As the men were preparing to portage their canoes around the Great Falls of the Missouri River, Sacagawea fell extremely ill with a high fever and severe pain in her lower abdomen. "[O]ur Intrepters wife verry Sick," noted Sergeant John Ordway in his journal. One of the most common medical treatments of that

Benjamin Rush (1745–1813), shown in this oil painting by Charles Willson Peale, was the renowned Philadelphian physician who helped train Meriwether Lewis for the expedition. The doctor strongly advocated "bleeding," or blood-letting, as a cure for many diseases. Both Lewis and Clark used the procedure on Sacagawea when she became seriously ill.

Pompy's "Bier"

While walking next to the Great Falls in late June, Clark, Sacagawea, Charbonneau, and 4-month-old Jean Baptiste took shelter from a heavy rain in a deep, dry ravine. Suddenly waters from a flash flood poured into the gully. Lewis described how Sacagawea almost lost her child that day: "The bier in which the woman carrys her child and all it's cloaths wer swept away as they lay at her feet she having time only to grasp her child."

Historians don't agree on what the "bier" used to carry Pompy actually was. Shoshone women would carry their infants using a wooden cradleboard, while Hidatsa babies were slung from the shoulder. Sacagawea could

(Above) This statue, by Pat Mathisen, depicts Pompy being carried in a Shoshone-style cradleboard. (Right) This sculpture by Leonard Crunelle shows Sacagawea using the Hidatsa-style sling to carry her son.

have followed either custom. As a result, artist's depictions of Sacagawea have shown both ways. In other mentions of a "bier" that occur in the journals, the men are referring to the mosquito netting used to protect them from insects.

time was "bleeding"—making a small cut in a patient's vein to remove the " bad blood" that was thought to be making the person ill. Clark did this procedure twice. It did not help.

Clark tried other treatments. Believing Sacagawea's bowels were obstructed, he gave her a laxative, but it did not resolve the pain in her abdomen. In an attempt to reduce her fever, Clark gave the young woman Peruvian bark tea. He also made a poultice from the bark and applied it to the painful area of her abdomen.

Upon his return to the main party on June 16, Lewis found Sacagawea very ill: "her pulse were scarcely perceptible, very quick frequently irregular and attended with strong nervous symptoms, that of the twitching of the fingers and . . . the arm," he wrote in his journal that day. Lewis continued the treatment with bark poultices. He also gave Sacagawea opium and laudanum (a mixture of opium and alcohol) to relieve her pain.

What seemed to help Sacagawea most was drinking water from a "Sulpher spring" that some of the men had found nearby. She began to recover, and by June 20 she was able to walk about.

FAMILIAR TERRITORY

In mid-July, the expedition completed the portage around the falls and continued on up the Missouri River. Finally, on July 22, near the present-day city of Helena, Montana, Sacagawea recognized a familiar landscape. Sergeant Gass wrote in his journal that day: "At breakfast our squaw informed us she had been at this place before when small." This information boosted the morale of the men—they were getting closer to Shoshone country.

This sketch from the Lewis and Clark journals shows the Great Falls of the Missouri and the 18-mile portage path the expedition took around them. The captains had known about only one set of falls and had figured they would need only two days to travel around it. However, they found five falls, as well as strong rapids and cascades, and a slope rising about 500 feet. Portaging the Great Falls would take a month to complete.

On July 27 the main party of the Corps of Discovery reached the Three Forks of the Missouri, the site where Sacagawea's life with her own people suddenly ended five years before. After giving names to the three tributaries, Lewis and Clark decided to follow the westernmost waterway, which they called Jefferson's River.

The shallow Jefferson ran swift, clear, and cold, and the members of the Corps of Discovery struggled to make headway against the current. Strong rapids forced the men to get into the river and pull and push the canoes upstream. In the August 5 entry of his journal, Sergeant Ordway described the harsh conditions:

> [T]he bottom of the River [is] covred with Slippery Small Stone and gravvel. . . . it is with difficulty & hard fatigue we git up them.

FINDING SACAGAWEA'S PEOPLE

As the members of the expedition struggled up Jefferson's River, Sacagawea's eyes searched for familiar landmarks. Finally, on August 8, she spied the Beaverhead, a hill that resembled the flat head of a swimming beaver. She knew that her people could not be far away. Captain Lewis reported in his journal that day:

> [T]he Indian woman recognized the point of a high plain to our right which she informed us was not very distant from the summer retreat of her nation on a river beyond the mountains which runs to the west.

SEARCHING FOR THE SHOSHONE

The Shoshone should still be fishing for salmon in the river, Sacagawea told Lewis, but the time for the annual

Sacagawea knew she was in familiar territory when she spotted the landmark her people called Beaverhead Rock. This natural formation is located north of present-day Dillon, Montana.

buffalo hunt was drawing near. The tribe would be easy to find if they were fishing: just search the river! But if the Shoshone had gone to hunt buffalo, they could be just about anywhere.

At this point in the Jefferson River, the waterway was growing more and more shallow, as it meandered all over a broad valley. The men were wading in cold water, dragging a half a dozen dugout canoes up a shallow, crooked river. Five miles of travel on the river was equivalent to just two miles of walking along a straight path. Lewis and Clark realized that a small party on foot could travel faster and farther, as much as 20 to 30 miles a day.

The day after Sacagawea identified the Beaverhead landmark, Captain Meriwether Lewis, George Drouillard, John Shields, and Hugh McNeal set off on foot to find the Shoshone. The Corps was nearing the Continental Divide and would require help to cross it. Their canoes contained several tons of baggage—more weight than the men could possibly carry on their backs. They needed horses, and the Shoshones had them. "[I]t is now all important with us to meet with those people [the Shoshones] as soon as possible," wrote Lewis before he left.

FATIGUE AND HUNGER

Meanwhile, the rest of the party remained with the canoes, slowly working their way up the cold, swift-moving river. The men endured grueling conditions. Rocks cut and bruised their feet, while heavy rains and hail pelted them. As the Corps of Discovery traveled deeper into the

Buffalo hunting season for the Shoshone typically took place in the fall. In mid-August, when the Lewis and Clark Expedition finally made contact with the tribe, its members were preparing to leave for the buffalo plains of today's Wyoming and Montana.

mountains, its members were eating about half what they were accustomed to as game was growing increasingly scarce. On August 15, Captain Clark wrote:

> [T]he men Complain much of their fatigue and being repetiedly in the water which weakens them much perticularly as they are obliged to live on pore Deer meet which has a Singular bitter taste.

Even when deer could be hunted, the venison had an unpleasant taste, apparently because the animals foraged on bitter foods. The same day he described the men's complaints, a worried Clark also noted that several days had passed since Lewis left: "I have no accounts of Capt Lewis Sence he Set out."

WAITING FOR LEWIS

On the afternoon of August 16, two hunters Clark had sent ahead returned to report that the river forked a few miles ahead, and that both forks were very shallow. If the canoes managed to reach this area tomorrow, the water would not be deep enough to push the boats any farther.

The two scouts reported that they had seen no sign of Lewis or his men. And now the need for horses was even more pressing. The expedition would not be able to travel any further without horses to carry some of the provisions and gear.

Nor could Corps remain where they were. Because game was scarce they would soon starve. Or they might freeze. The cold mornings were warnings that winter would come early to these mountains. In his journal entry of August 17, Sergeant John Ordway observed how the weather had changed:

> [A] clear cold morning. we have been cold this
> Several nights under 2 blankets or Robes, over us.
> a little white frost the air chilley & cold.

That morning, after a cold breakfast of currants, serviceberries, and leftover venison, the men eased back into the chilly river to force the canoes upstream once more. Sacagawea slung her baby on her back and with her husband continued the journey along the river by foot. Clark followed behind.

"MY PEOPLE!"

Sacagawea and Charbonneau had walked no more than a mile when several men on horses rode into view. One of the riders was George Drouillard. The others were Shoshone warriors. Sacagawea danced for joy when she saw them. She turned back to Clark. Pointing toward the riders with her left hand, she sucked the fingers of her right hand. This was sign language for "my people!"

Lewis had sent Drouillard ahead to find the main party and direct them to the camp at the river fork where Lewis and the rest of the Shoshones were waiting. "There were about 20 of the natives came over with Captain Lewis," Patrick Gass would write later in his journal.

As Clark, Sacagawea, and Charbonneau approached the camp, a Shoshone woman came out to greet Sacagawea. It was her friend, the girl who had escaped capture when Sacagawea was taken by the Hidatsa. Sacagawea had never known if her friend had reached home safely. Her friend could not have expected that she

Lewis's First Meeting with the Shoshone

On August 12, Lewis and his three men crossed the Continental Divide at Lemhi Pass. The following day, they came upon three Shoshone women gathering food a few miles from their village. One of the women fled, but the two others froze in fear, certain they would be killed. Instead, they received reassurances from Lewis, who laid down his gun and gave them beads, moccasin awls, and small mirrors. Lewis won their confidence when he painted their cheeks with bright red paint, or vermilion—an act Sacagawea had advised him to do because it signified that he came in peace.

Soon a war party of 60 Shoshone appeared, but the Shoshone women explained that the newcomers were friendly. Through Plains Indian sign language, which Drouillard knew, Lewis explained that his group wanted to buy some of their horses. He also promised to open up trade with the Shoshone so they could acquire the guns they wanted to defend themselves against their enemies.

The Shoshone chief, Cameahwait, agreed to bring a group of his warriors and accompany Lewis back across the Continental Divide to the forks of the Jefferson River. There, Lewis had arranged to reunite with the main party of the expedition. On August 16, Captain Lewis wrote:

> I had mentioned to the chief several times that we had with us a woman of his nation who had been taken prisoner by the [Hidatsa], and that by means of her I hoped to explain myself more fully than I could do [by] signs.

A Charles M. Russell painting depicting the Lewis and Clark Expedition meeting the Shoshone. On the right, Sacagawea hugs her childhood friend in greeting.

would ever see Sacagawea again. Their joyous reunion was very emotional, wrote Lewis.

CAMP FORTUNATE

Later in the day, a council between the captains and the Shoshone was held at the camp, under the shade of a canopy of willows and a canoe canvas sail. Lewis later reported,

> [A]bout 4 P.M. we called them together and through the medium of Labuish, Charbono and Sah-cah-gar-weah, we communicated to them fully the objects which had brought us into this distant part of the country in which we took care to make them a conspicuous object of our own good wishes and the care of our government.

FROM THE KNIFE RIVER VILLAGES TO CAMP FORTUNATE

BRITISH POSSESSIONS

Lake Manitob

Marias R.

Missouri R.

LEWIS AND CLARK 1805

Great Falls Portage

Musselshell R.

Three Forks of the Missouri

Yellowstone R.

Beaverhead Rock

Camp Fortunate

Lemhi Pass

Jefferson R.

Madison R.

Gallatin R.

Hidatsa Villages

Fort Mandan

Knife R.

Mandan Villages

Arikara Villages

R o c k y

Wind R.

Bighorn R.

CONTINENTAL

DIVIDE

OREGON

COUNTRY

Snake R.

G r e a t   P l a i n s

Niobrara R.

Great Salt Lake

M o u n t a i n s

LOUISIANA

TERRITORY

N. Platte R.

S. Platte R.

Platte

SPANISH

POSSESSIONS

Missouri R.

Before the council began, however, Sacagawea looked at the Shoshone chief, Cameahwait, and recognized him as her brother. She jumped up, embraced him, and wept for joy. They spoke for some time before returning to the council. During the course of the meeting, Sacagawea's emotions overcame her several more times and she broke down in tears.

Buying horses from the Shoshone was a major topic of discussion. On August 12, as he had crossed the Continental Divide at a site now known as Lemhi Pass, Lewis had discovered that many more barriers lay to the west. He reported in his journal that day that he and his men had seen "immence ranges of high mountains still to the West of us with their tops partially covered with snow."

Lewis realized that the Corps of Discovery needed horses not only to carry their baggage over the divide, but also to continue their journey west through the mountains. The Corps needed help from the Indians, as well as horses, especially a guide to direct them through the mountains. During the council, the Shoshone agreed to all of these requests. Lewis and Clark were so pleased with the results of the meeting that they named the site Camp Fortunate.

However, Sacagawea's joyous reunion with her brother was also shadowed by grief. When the council ended, she learned sad news: all the members of her family were dead except for two brothers and a son of her eldest sister, a small boy.

7

ON TO THE PACIFIC

When he first visited the Shoshone camp, Lewis quickly saw that the nearby Lemhi River was too shallow for canoes. Chief Cameahwait told Lewis that the Lemhi flowed into a larger river, known today as the Salmon River. Although the Salmon River led to the Columbia River, it was not navigable by canoe because it had many rapids.

This information didn't sound promising, but Lewis and Clark decided that one of them should examine the Salmon River more closely before they completely ruled it out as a route to the west. Finding a navigable river flowing west remained their most important goal.

THE LEMHI VALLEY

During the council at Camp Fortunate, Lewis and Clark had determined a strategy. Clark would leave right away with a Shoshone guide and crew of men to scout the Salmon River. If the river looked suitable, the men with

Clark would begin making canoes. Meanwhile, Lewis and the others would remain at Camp Fortunate to prepare the Corps' baggage for the portage across Lemhi Pass. Preparations included burying the belongings they couldn't carry and hiding the canoes.

On August 18, Sacagawea, her son, Charbonneau, and most of the Shoshones went with Clark across the Lemhi Pass to the Shoshone camp in the Lemhi Valley. From there, Clark and his men continued on toward the Salmon River, accompanied by the Shoshone guide, whom the Corps of Discovery had nicknamed Old Toby.

Meanwhile, at the tribe's village, Sacagawea and Cameahwait told the Shoshones that the explorers would pay them for the use of their horses and for assistance in

The friendly relationship between Lewis and the Shoshone had been cemented when he first met the Indians and participated in a pipe-smoking ritual with their chief. This image from Lewis's August 13, 1805, journal entry shows a detailed description of the ceremony and a sketch of the Shoshone "peace pipe."

carrying the expedition's baggage across the divide. A few days later, the Shoshones who were willing to help set off to Camp Fortunate with the Charbonneau family.

AVERTING DISASTER

At the camp, the baggage was loaded on the horses. Then the main party of the expedition set out for Lemhi Pass. However, as the group was traveling through the mountains on the morning of August 25, Sacagawea learned that Cameahwait had sent a messenger back to the Shoshone

In late August the main party of the Lewis and Clark Expedition crossed the Continental Divide through the Lemhi Pass, in the Beaverhead Mountains. These mountains make up the southern portion of the Bitteroot Range.

camp in the Lemhi Valley. His instructions were that his people should pack their baggage and begin journeying east for the buffalo hunt. Cameahwait and the Shoshones with him would join them, taking the horses they had allowed the explorers to use for portaging Lemhi pass.

Sacagawea realized that without horses the Corps of Discovery would be left stranded in the mountains. She told Charbonneau to inform Lewis of Cameahwait's plans, but for some reason her husband waited for several hours before telling the captain. When Lewis learned of Charbonneau's delay in passing along such vital information, he was furious. That day, he wrote angrily in his journal:

> [A]ltho' [Charbonneau] had been in possession of this information since early in the morning when it had been communicated to him by his Indian woman yet he never mentioned it untill the after noon. I could not forbear speaking to him with some degree of asperity.

Lewis, like Sacagawea, realized that Cameahwait's decision would mean the expedition would go no farther. He spoke with the chief. Was it true, he asked, that he had sent such an order? Cameahwait said that he had done so because his people were hungry. They didn't have enough food to eat and winter was coming. They needed to leave to hunt buffalo. Lewis finally convinced the chief to stick with his agreement to help the explorers, and he gave the Shoshones most of the food the Corps had.

AN ALTERNATIVE ROUTE

As soon as he arrived at the Shoshone village on August 26, Lewis received a message from Clark that the swift-moving Salmon River was too dangerous to serve as a route to the

Pacific. But Clark's Shoshone guide was willing to take the expedition west by an alternative route. There was a trail to the north, over the Bitterroot Mountains, that would take them to a passable tributary—the Clearwater River. This river was navigable, and it eventually flowed into the Columbia River.

The expedition would need to buy horses to use for this journey. With Sacagawea providing assistance as an interpreter, Lewis and Clark purchased 30 horses from the Shoshones. Although the horses were intended mostly for carrying gear and provisions, one was set aside for Sacagawea to ride. Lewis had given Charbonneau some trade goods to buy a horse for her use.

On August 30, the Lewis Clark Expedition set off on foot, leading their Shoshone packhorses. As they ascended the North Fork of the Salmon River, their Indian guide Toby led them through rough country where there was no trail.

After reaching the Bitterroot River Valley, near present-day Sula, Montana, the Corps met a band of the Salish tribe, who were friends of the Shoshone. A Shoshone boy living with the Salish helped Sacagawea interpret for the expedition, so Lewis and Clark were able to purchase fresh horses.

Lewis and Clark saw their first Pacific salmon when they reached the Lemhi River, which was teeming with spawning fish. Biologists estimate that in the early 1800s about 10 to 16 million salmon and steelhead migrated each year along the Columbia River system from the Pacific Ocean. Today, most water of the Lemhi is used for irrigation purposes, and only a few hundred salmon return to the river each summer.

O nly about a mile separated the streams leading to the Missouri from the headwaters of the Columbia. Although it was not possible to navigate these upper waterways by canoe, one could walk from one river system source to the other, as John Ordway reported on August 26, 1805:

> [W]e passed a nomber of large Springs and I drank at the head Spring of the Missourie ran South & walked across a ridge only about one mile and drank at the head Spring of the Columbian River running west.

THROUGH THE BITTERROOT MOUNTAINS

The Corps traveled down the Bitterroot River to the Lolo Trail, just south of present-day Missoula, Montana. In order to allow everyone to rest for the upcoming journey over the Bitterroot Mountains, the captains decided to establish a temporary camp, which they called Traveler's Rest. While there, Toby informed Lewis and Clark that the journey from the Great Falls of the Missouri to Traveler's Rest would have taken just 4 days if they had walked overland. Because the expedition followed the winding Missouri River, the trip had taken 53 days.

The following day, on September 11, the Corps headed west into the mountains. They now had a trail to follow—the path used by the Nez Perce Indians when the tribe went east to hunt buffalo on the plains.

The members of the expedition traveled under punishing conditions, walking for many days along high ridges and narrow, rocky trails. No matter where they looked, all they saw were mountains. Because there was little game, they suffered from hunger. It rained and snowed, making the trails

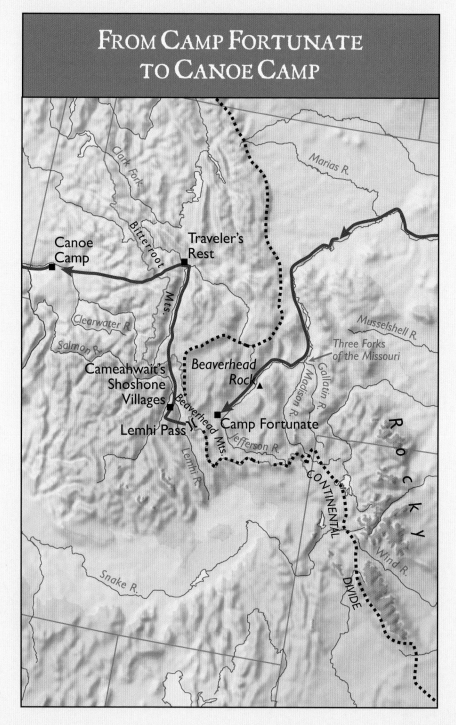

FROM CAMP FORTUNATE
TO CANOE CAMP

wet and slippery. In the September 16, 1805, entry of his journal Clark reported:

> I have been wet and as cold in every part as I ever was in my life, indeed I was at one time fearfull my feet would freeze in the thin mockersons which I wore.

Old Toby lost the trail, which added a couple of days to the journey. The difficult weather conditions also slowed their progress so that a crossing that should have taken five days took eleven.

THE NEZ PERCE

By the time the expedition left the mountains, on September 22, its members were in terrible shape. They finally reached the village of the hospitable Nez Perce, who gave them dried salmon and camas root to eat. Unfortunately, the sudden change in diet made them sick to their stomach. Clark wrote:

> [The Nez Perce] gave us a Small piece of Buffalow meat, Some dried Salmon beries & roots in differ-ent States . . . I find myself very unwell all evening from eating the fish and roots too freely.

Native to western North America, camas is also known as quamash or wild hyacinth. It was a valuable food source to the Nez Perce and many other tribes, who harvested the bulbs of the blue-flowered perennial in the summer and autumn. The bulbs could be eaten raw, boiled into a kind of soup, or pit-roasted. The slow roasting process resulted in sweet and nutritious food source, similar in taste to that of a sweet potato.

Sacagawea wasn't the only Indian woman to help the expedition. Nez Perce oral tradition says that the tribe considered killing the members of the Corps of Discovery, but was persuaded to treat them hospitably by an elderly Nez Perce woman named Watkuweis. She had been befriended by whites when she was a captive of a tribe living to the east.

The men recovered slowly, their spirits boosted by the sight of the Clearwater River and the tall, straight ponderosa pine trees that grew along its banks. In their weakened state, the men were not up to hollowing out tree trunks to make canoes to take them on the next stage of their journey. However, the Nez Perce showed them another technique for making canoes—using fire instead of tools.

Lewis and Clark told the Indians that the Corps planned to return the following spring, and the tribe agreed to look after their horses. The Nez Perce chief, Twisted Hair, drew a map on white elkskin of the rivers toward the west and directed the captains to follow the Clearwater to the Snake River and from there, on to the Columbia.

BACK TO CANOES

By October 7, the men had completed five new canoes, and were ready to set off. Once back on the water, they experienced for the first time in two years the luxury of flowing with the current, rather than fighting against it.

As the Corps of Discovery paddled down the tributaries of the Columbia, they noted that the land surrounding them supported little vegetation and that hunting was poor. However, the rivers teemed with millions of fish, which supported the large Indian population in the region.

*The confluence of the Snake (Lewis's River) and Columbia Rivers, as depicted
in the Lewis and Clark journals. On October 16, the expedition portaged
around a set of rapids on the Snake, and finally arrived at the Columbia,
which they also referred to as the "Great River of the West."*

In this 1905 painting of the Lewis and Clark Expedition near the mouth of the Columbia River, artist Charles M. Russell shows Sacagawea communicating with Chinook Indians using sign language. (Inset) Lewis and Clark gave detailed descriptions and illustrations of the various kinds of Chinook canoes in their journals. The canoe with the high bow (front) is similar to the one illustrated by Russell in the painting.

In this part of the land, the expedition members met new tribes almost every day.

Soon the group left behind a dry, desert region and entered lush evergreen rainforests. In this forested area, the average rainfall was nearly five times that of the plains. One of the tribes living in this region was the Chinook, who constructed impressive, seaworthy canoes, unlike the crude canoes made by the Corps of Discovery.

"A TOKEN OF PEACE"

As ambassadors of President Thomas Jefferson, Lewis and Clark visited many of the tribes. Some of the natives were frightened at the sight of well-armed white men coming down the river toward them.

But, as William Clark wrote on October 13, 1805, the presence of Sacagawea and her son made a difference:

> The wife of Shabono [Charbonneau] our inter-
> petr we find reconsiles all the Indians, as to our
> friendly intentions a woman with a party of men is
> a token of peace.

The men of the Corps of Discovery were not viewed as dangerous, because no war party included women and children.

8

WAITING OUT THE WINTER

On November 7, the Corps reached the broad estuary of the great Columbia River. Lewis and Clark believed they had finally reached the Pacific Ocean; however, the canoes were actually still about 20 miles away from the sea.

High winds and rough seas kept the expedition from making progress, and several members of the party, including Sacagawea, became violently ill from seasickness. Rain fell for eleven days in a row, Clark noted in his journal, and the group was pinned at a campsite on the northern shore of the Columbia. The continuously damp weather rotted their leather bedding and clothing, and the poor weather made hunting difficult.

CHOOSING WINTER QUARTERS

On November 24 Lewis and Clark decided to call the group together to take an opinion poll. It was obvious they could not spend the winter where they were. They needed

The sun sets over the Pacific Ocean. "Ocian in view! O! the joy," Captain William Clark wrote ecstatically on November 7, 1805, when the canoes reached the Columbia River estuary. It would actually be another two weeks before the Corps reached the shoreline of the Pacific.

to set up winter camp. The two most popular choices were to go back up the Columbia River or to cross the bay to the south side and seek a more sheltered location. Every member of the expedition expressed his or her choice, which Clark recorded.

For Sacagawea's vote, Clark wrote, "Janey in favour of a place where there is plenty of Potas." The name "Janey" had not appeared in any journal entry before now, and is presumed to be a nickname either her husband or Clark had given her. "Potas" came from the wapato, a plant with potato-like roots that grew in the area. "Cross the river" got the most votes, and so men were sent out to find a good site on the south side of the Columbia.

By the time that the Lewis and Clark Expedition arrived in the North Pacific region, the tribes living along the western coast were experienced in trading with whites who had already visited the region by ship. So when the Clatsop visited the Corps' campsite on November 20, the Indians struck a hard bargain. One of the Indians wore a sea otter robe that Lewis and Clark wanted to purchase as a gift for President Jefferson. However, nothing they offered to trade was acceptable. Clark's entry on that date reports:

> [O]ne of the Indians had on a roab made of 2 Sea Otter Skins the fur of them were more butifull than any fur I had ever Seen both Capt. Lewis & my Self endeavored to purchase the *roab* with differant articles at length we precured it for a belt of blue beeds which the Squar—wife of our interpreter Shabono wore around her waste.

Sacagawea made the trade possible. In exchange for agreeing to give up her blue beaded belt, she later received "a Coate of Blue Cloth" from Lewis and Clark.

On December 5, Sergeant Gass noted that Lewis and a scouting party had found a good spot:

> They have found a place . . . up a small river which puts into a large bay on the south side of the Columbia, that will answer very well for winter quarters, as game is very plenty, which is the main object for us; and we intend to move there. . . . There is more wet weather on this coast, than I ever knew in any other place; during a month we have had but 3 fair days; and there is no prospect of a change.

The Corps found a suitable location on a small river near present-day Astoria, Oregon, where they built their winter quarters, Fort Clatsop—named for the local tribe. The eight cabins and stockade were completed in time for the members of the expedition to move in and celebrate Christmas. Clark reported that among the gifts given during the holiday were two dozen white weasel tails, presented by Sacagawea to him. Shoshone men often used the tails to decorate the edges of otter pelts.

The weather of the present-day Oregon coast was as wet as the North Dakota climate had been cold. Almost every day it would rain, snow, sleet, or hail.

JOURNEY TO "THE GREAT WATERS"

The staple diet that winter was elk, but the damp weather often spoiled the meat before the hunters could get it to

Once a site for a permanent winter quarters was chosen, the men of Corps of Discovery began building the shelter to protect them from the incessant rain. This image from the journal of Patrick Gass shows "Captain Clark and his men building a line of huts," typical of the winter forts built by the expedition.

A replica of Fort Clatsop stands near modern-day Astoria, Oregon. Named in honor of the local Clatsop Indians, the fort was ready to shelter the 33 members of the expedition by late December.

the fort. When the natives brought news that a whale had washed up onshore to their south, Clark organized a trip to obtain some of the meat and blubber. The route to the seacoast would be difficult, so Clark did not intend to take the Charbonneau family. That was a mistake, Clark reported in his January 6, 1806, journal entry:

> Shabono and his Indian woman was very impatient to be permitted to go with me, and was therefore indulged; She observed that She had traveled a long way with us to See the great waters, and that now that monstrous fish was also to be Seen, She thought it verry hard that She Could not be permitted to See either.

Fort Clatsop was several miles from the coast, so Sacagawea had not seen the sandy beaches, dramatic rock formations, and the great waves rolling in from the Pacific. Clark relented, and so Sacagawea, Pompy, and Charbonneau joined the 13-member party that day as it set out for the coast.

The most difficult part of the trip to the ocean was scaling the thousand-foot high Tillamook Head, a mountain cliff on the coast between present-day Seaside and Cannon Beach, Oregon. Clark would later describe Tillamook Head as "the Steepest worst & highest mountain I ever assended." At least a hundred feet of the mountain was so sheer that the hikers had to pull themselves up by grabbing on to shrubs and roots.

Two days later, when the party got to the 105-foot-long whale carcass, they found that it had already been

During their trek to see the great whale that had washed up on the coast of the Pacific, Sacagawea and the other members of the Corps passed by this 235-foot high rock, known today as Haystack Rock. It is located on Cannon Beach, Oregon.

FROM CANOE CAMP
TO THE PACIFIC

Mt. Rainier

Cascade Range

Columbia R.

Clark Fork

Fort Clatsop
Salt Camp
Tillamook Head
Whale Site

Columbia R.

LEWIS AND CLARK 1805

Canoe
Camp

Bitterroot Mts.

Mt. Hood

Willamette R.

Clearwater R.

Salmon R.

Snake R.

Cameahwait's
Shoshone
Villages

Lemhi Pass

Lemhi R.

OREGON

COUNTRY

NATURAL

Snake R.

SPANISH POSSESSIONS

Great Salt
Lake

Sie

stripped clean by the local Indians, the Tillamook. The Corps traded with the Tillamook, obtaining 300 pounds of blubber and a few gallons of whale oil for their use. After camping for the night on the beach, the party set out the next day to return back to the fort.

WINTERING AT FORT CLATSOP

The days passed slowly at Fort Clatsop, with everybody confined by the weather to their smoky, flea-infested cabins. Lewis and Clark spent their time writing and drawing maps from the notes and sketches they had made since leaving Fort Mandan in April. They wrote long journal entries describing the cultures of the coastal tribes and the new plants and animals they had encountered.

The other men occupied themselves with gathering firewood and hunting elk and other game, using the tanned skins to make clothing to replace garments and moccasins that were falling apart. To keep the meat from spoiling, the men dried it in a smoke house or preserved it with salt. Lewis and Clark had established a small camp on the seacoast, where the men kept large kettles of ocean water boiling day and night, producing large quantities of salt.

THE JOURNEY HOME BEGINS

As the food supply dwindled and the explorers grew increasingly intolerant of the poor weather, everyone agreed that they would leave as soon as possible. On March 23, 1806, they set off up the Columbia River, eager to leave Fort Clatsop behind. Once again they were fighting upstream in a large river, but now they knew that each stroke of the paddle took them closer to home.

Around mid-April the Corps determined that they had enough of the Columbia River. They began to trade their

On March 23, 1806, the Lewis and Clark Expedition began the journey back home by canoe. This 1906 drawing by Frederic Remington shows Lewis and Clark in canoes at the mouth of the Columbia River.

boats for horses as they continued traveling up the Columbia, by land and water. By the time the members of the expedition reached the Snake River, they were able to leave the canoes and head overland with their horses.

THE WALLA WALLA

Near the confluence of the Snake and Columbia Rivers, the group stopped for a short visit with the Walla Walla tribe. The tribe's chief, Yellepit, welcomed the expedition. He had been disappointed the previous fall when the Corps had passed through the region but not spent time with his people.

In his journal entry dated April 28, 1806, Lewis explained how Sacagawea served as an interpreter to help his party learn more about the Walla Walla people:

> [W]e found a Shoshone woman, prisoner among these people by means of whome and Sahcahgarweah we found the means of conversing with the Wollah-wollahs. [W]e conversed with them for several hours and fully satisfyed all their enquiries with rispect to ourselves and the objects of our pursuit.

ONCE AGAIN AMONG THE NEZ PERCE

Visiting the Walla Walla at the same time were some Nez Perce people, who offered to guide the Corps back to their village on the Clearwater River. The Corps gladly accepted the offer. It was almost May. They hoped that with luck they would be able to recover the horses they had left with the Nez Perce, cross the Rocky Mountains, and start down the Missouri River before summer began.

But as the Corps reached the Clearwater River in mid-May, they saw that the mountains on the distant eastern horizon were still snow-covered. Spring was late in coming to the Rocky Mountains, and the pass was blocked. The members of the expedition set up camp at present-day Kamiah, Idaho. Here, they waited for a month for the snow to melt in mountains.

During that time, they visited frequently with the Nez Perce. In a stroke of good luck, they found a young Shoshone man living with the tribe. He had learned enough of the Nez Perce language to allow Lewis and Clark to again enlist Sacagawea's services as an interpreter.

The Corps bought roots from the Nez Perce, including the camas root that had made them sick the year before. Sacagawea recognized another plant, whose roots the Shoshone ate to lessen the bloating, cramps and intestinal gas caused by camas. Lewis found the roots of this plant, a kind of wild fennel, to be "very agreeable food . . . they dispell the wind which [camas is] apt to create."

THE CORPS DIVIDES

By late June, the Corps was finally able to cross the Bitterroots. There was still much snow on parts of the trail, but several young Nez Perce men helped the Corps stay on the correct trail. After crossing the mountains, the party camped again at Traveler's Rest. At that time, Lewis and Clark decided that the Corps would split into two detachments.

Lewis's detachment would head to the Great Falls of the Missouri River. However, this time the group would travel overland, rather than follow the winding route of the upper Missouri. After reaching the falls, Lewis would explore to the north, along the Marias River with a small party while the rest of his men recovered the goods they had hidden when they portaged around the falls the previous June.

Meanwhile, Clark's detachment would return to Camp Fortunate, on the upper forks of the Jefferson River, where the expedition had left the canoes in August 1805. From there, Clark's party would divide again: Some of his men, led by Sergeant Ordway, would take the canoes downriver, portage them around the Great Falls of the Missouri, and meet Lewis's men. Clark would take the rest of his group to explore along the Yellowstone River.

On July 3, Lewis and Clark parted from Traveler's Rest, with the understanding that they would meet up again with each other near the confluence of the Missouri and Yellowstone Rivers. Sacagawea, Charbonneau, and Pompy accompanied Clark, who wanted to use their translating skills to speak with the Crow Indians who lived in the area he planned to explore, as well as with Shoshones. His entry for that day reads:

> I took My leave of Capt Lewis and the indians and at 8 A M Set out with . . . interpreter Shabono & his wife & child (as an interpreter & interpretess for the Crow Inds and the latter for the Shoshoni) with 50 horses.

9

"A Pilot Through This Country"

Clark's detachment soon reached the place where members of the expedition had encountered the Salish the previous September, in the southern Bitterroot Valley. While scouting possible routes, one of Clark's men, John Shields, found the trail the Salish used to cross the Continental Divide when they went to hunt buffalo. The pass that Clark's party traveled through in July 1806 is known today as Gibbon's Pass, which is located in southwestern Montana.

"A Pilot Through This Country"

After Clark's party crossed the divide, the group entered a large valley known today as the Big Hole Valley. In his July 6 journal entry, Clark described the valley in great detail:

Sacagawea points the way for Clark in this painting by N. C. Wyeth. It was while Clark's party was journeying across the plains to the Yellowstone River that Clark recognized the Indian woman for her services as a pilot, or guide. Sacagawea knew the land, having traveled frequently through it as a child during Shoshone food-gathering expeditions.

> [W]e assended a Small rise and beheld an open boutifull Leavel Vally or plain of about 20 Miles wide and near 60 long extending N & S. in every direction around which I could see high points of Mountains Covered with Snow.

It was here that Sacagawea truly became a guide for the first time. "[O]ur Intrepters wife tells us that . . . She knows the country," wrote Sgt. John Ordway. The following August, Lewis would hear the story and note in his journal why Sacagawea was so familiar with the region:

[Sacagawea] recognised the plain immediately. She had travelled it often during her childhood, and informed us that it was the great resort of the Shoshonees, who came for the purpose of gathering quamash [camas] and cows [kouse], and of taking beaver, with which the plain abounded.

Sacagawea pointed out to Clark and his men a shortcut to the southeast, through the mountains. Two days later Clark's party reached Camp Fortunate and the upper branches of the Jefferson River.

The party arrived to find all but one of the seven canoes in usable condition. Some of the men took the canoes down Jefferson's River, while the rest of Clark's party accompanied them on horseback.

When the group reached the Three Forks of the Missouri, Clark ordered Sgt. Ordway and ten men to continue down the Missouri and portage the canoes around the Great Falls and meet up with Lewis's detachment. Meanwhile, Clark, Sacagawea, Pompy, Charbonneau, and the rest of the men rode east toward the Yellowstone River.

On July 13 Sacagawea directed the group to a trail the Shoshones used when they went to hunt bison along the

Sacagawea was familiar with the Big Hole Valley because her people would travel to the area in the spring months of April and May to harvest the tuberous roots of kouse, a parsnip-like plant that grew in abundance there. Also known as biscuitroot, kouse was eaten fresh or dried and ground into a meal, mixed with water, and baked into cakes.

While Lewis's party explored near the Marias River, the men got into a fight with several Blackfeet when the warriors tried to steal the party's guns and horses. The incident resulted in the only bloodshed to occur between the expedition and native tribes. Patrick Gass's journal illustrated the encounter in which two Blackfeet Indians died.

Yellowstone River. Clark's journal entry made that day praises her usefulness as a guide in the region:

> [T]he indian woman who has been of great Service to me as a pilot through this Country recommends a gap in the mountain more South which I shall cross.

Two days later the group crossed through the pass between the Three Forks of the Missouri and the Yellowstone that she had pointed out, now known as Bozeman Pass. When the party reached the Yellowstone, the men stopped to construct canoes so they could continue by water down the river. The cottonwood trees available along the river were fairly small, so the men hollowed out two trunks to make two small canoes, which were then lashed together to make them stable.

Less than two weeks later, on July 25, Clark's party came upon a 200-foot-high rock outcropping along the river, located northeast of present-day Billings, Montana. Some members of the party climbed the butte and discovered Indian petroglyphs carved in the soft sandstone. Clark was inspired to carve his own name and the date on the face of the rock. He named the butte Pompy's Tower in honor of Sacagawea's son, now an 18-month-old toddler. The landmark would later become known as Pompeys Pillar.

LEAVING THE EXPEDITION

On August 12, the Corps was reunited on the Missouri River when Lewis's detachment joined Clark's. Two days later the boats reached the Knife River villages. There, Lewis and Clark were disappointed to learn that a Hidatsa war party had attacked and killed members of the Shoshone shortly after the Corps of Discovery had left them in 1805. The captains had believed the Hidatsa would abide by their promise not to make war against other Indian tribes, in accordance with the wishes of Thomas Jefferson.

Lewis and Clark invited the Hidatsa and Mandan chiefs to join the Corps in its downstream voyage, so they could visit President Jefferson in Washington, D.C. A Mandan chief, Sheheke, agreed to join them. However, the Hidatsa chiefs declined the invitation because they were afraid that the Teton Sioux would kill them as they descended the Missouri River.

Since his services as a Hidatsa interpreter would not be needed, Charbonneau—as well as Sacagawea and their toddler—decided to leave the expedition and remain at Knife River. On August 17, Clark wrote,

> [W]e also took our leave of T. Chabono, his Snake Indian wife and their Son Child who had accompanied us on our rout to the pacific Ocean in the Capacity of interpreter and interpretes.

Pompy's Tower, known today as Pompeys Pillar, east of Billings, Montana. Located at a natural crossing of the river, the butte served as a meeting place for the Plains Indians, who painted pictographs and carved petroglyphs on its surface. (Inset) A protective cover shields William Clark's signature and the date of his visit—July 25, 1806—carved into the northeastern face of the butte. It is the only physical evidence along the route that remains today of the Lewis and Clark Expedition.

AN UNUSUAL OFFER

William Clark's journal entry at that time also notes how he offered to take Charbonneau and Sacagawea's "little Son," whom Clark described as "a butifull promising Child who is 19 months old." When he was old enough, his parents said, they would take him to Clark in St. Louis for him to raise, Clark wrote, "in Such a manner as I thought proper."

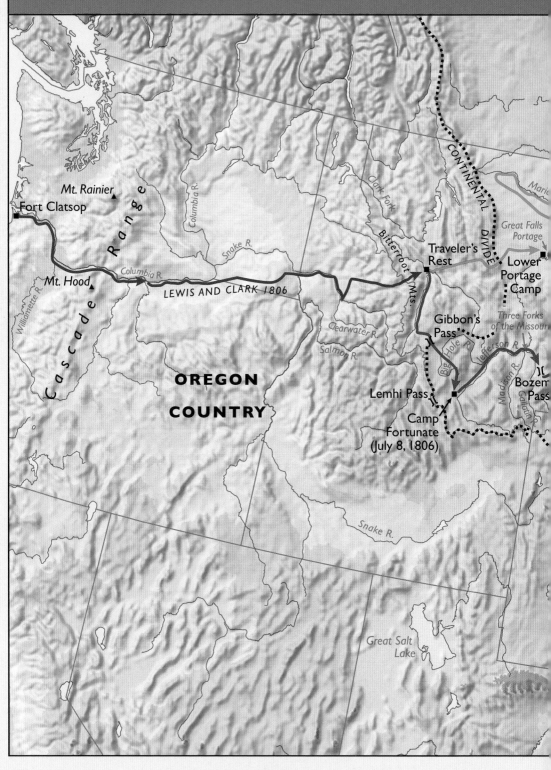

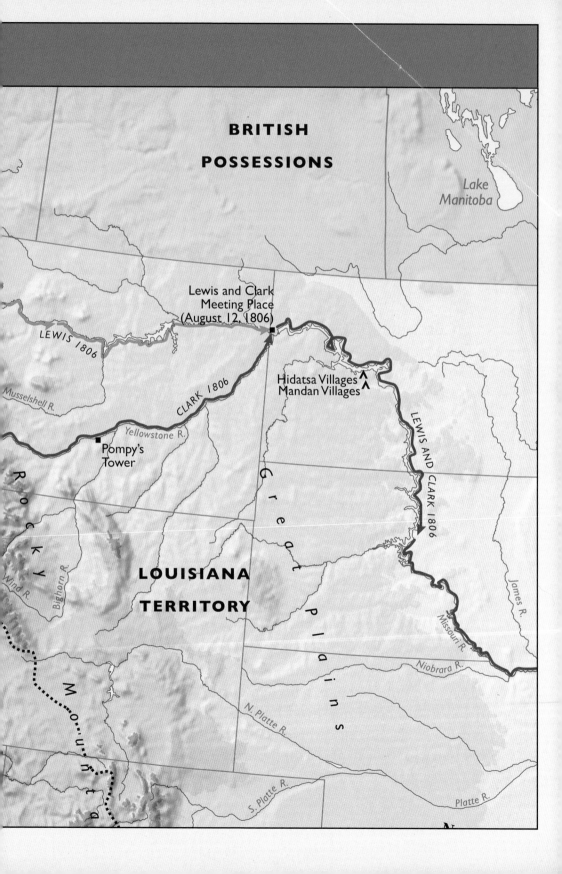

BRITISH

POSSESSIONS

Lake Manitoba

Lewis and Clark
Meeting Place
(August 12, 1806)

LEWIS 1806

CLARK 1806

Hidatsa Villages
Mandan Villages

Musselshell R.

Yellowstone R.

Pompy's
Tower

LEWIS AND CLARK 1806

R
o
c
k
y

Wind R.

Bighorn R.

LOUISIANA

TERRITORY

G
r
e
a
t

P
l
a
i
n
s

James R.

Missouri R.

Niobrara R.

M
o
u
n
t
a

N. Platte R.

S. Platte R.

Platte R.

Three days later, on August 20, Clark wrote a letter to Charbonneau in which he repeated his offer to raise Pomp:

> As to your little Son (my boy *Pomp*) you well know my fondness for him and my anxiety to take and raise him as my own child. I once more tell you if you will bring your son Baptiest to me I will educate him and treat him as my own child . . . Wishing you and your family great suckcess & with anxious expectations of seeing my little danceing boy Baptiest I shall remain your Friend.

In the letter, Clark also said he would help Charbonneau acquire a farm if he wanted to live in the St. Louis area, or if he wished to remain at Knife River, Clark would help him get a job as an Indian language interpreter for the United States. Long after the expedition ended, Clark would maintain his ties to the Charbonneau family.

IN ST. LOUIS

In March 1807, the U.S. Congress passed a bill to compensate former members of the expedition. It awarded 1,600 acres of land each to Lewis and Clark and 320 acres (130 hectares) each to the other members, including Charbonneau. Sacagawea did not receive any similar compensation.

Two years later, in the fall of 1809, Sacagawea traveled with her husband and four-year-old son to St. Louis, probably on the boat that returned to Knife River carrying the Mandan chief Sheheke, who had left in August 1806 with the Corps. The family lived for a time in St. Louis. While there, Charbonneau received land as further payment for his participation in the expedition. He chose property on the Missouri River, north of St. Louis.

The first public information about the Lewis and Clark Expedition appeared in Jefferson's Message, read in Congress on February 19, 1806, and subsequently published. It contained a detailed letter from Lewis and information on various Indian nations written before the expedition left Fort Mandan in April 1805. Jefferson's Message also contained reports from two men who had explored other parts of the Louisiana territory—John Sibley and William Dunbar.

MESSAGE

FROM THE

PRESIDENT OF THE UNITED STATES,

COMMUNICATING

DISCOVERIES

MADE IN EXPLORING

THE MISSOURI, RED RIVER AND WASHITA,

BY

CAPTAINS LEWIS AND CLARK, DOCTOR SIBLEY,

AND

MR. DUNBAR;

WITH

A STATISTICAL ACCOUNT

OF THE

COUNTRIES ADJACENT.

FEBRUARY 19, 1806.

Read, and ordered to lie on the table.

CITY OF WASHINGTON;

A. & G. WAY, PRINTERS.

1806.

However, the settled life did not agree with Charbonneau, and in the spring of 1811 he sold his land to Clark. After being hired by the Missouri Fur Company as an interpreter, Charbonneau headed back up the Missouri River with Sacagawea. Pomp, now six years old, remained behind in St. Louis to attend school.

One of the men traveling on the boat with Sacagawea and Charbonneau wrote in his journal that Toussaint had left St. Louis because he had "become weary of civilized life." The fellow passenger also described Sacagawea:

> The woman . . . of a mild and gentle disposition greatly attached to the whites, whose manners and dress she tries to imitate, but she has become sickly and longed to revisit her native country.

103

DEATH OF "THE WIFE OF CHARBONNEAU"

In August 1812, Sacagawea, Charbonneau, and their infant daughter were living at Fort Manuel, a Missouri Fur Company trading post located on the Missouri River, near present-day Kenel, South Dakota. Born sometime earlier in the year, the baby girl was named Lisette.

On December 20 of that year, John Luttig, a clerk at Fort Manuel, recorded a sad event in his journal:

> This Evening the Wife of Charbonneau a Snake Squaw, died of a putrid fever she was a good and the best Woman in the fort, aged about 25 years she left a fine infant girl.

Historians aren't certain what Luttig meant by "putrid fever." The term was sometimes used at that time to refer to a disease known today as typhus, a highly infectious bacterial disease spread by lice or fleas. Its symptoms include headache, chills, high fever, and severe muscular pain.

However, it is possible that Sacagawea died from another cause. The passenger accompanying her on the boat ride from St. Louis in the spring of 1811 had noted she was sickly then. And the fact that no one else at Fort Manuel seems to have suffered from typhus at that time makes it less likely that the disease caused Sacagawea's death.

SACAGAWEA'S CHILDREN

In March 1813, Fort Manuel was abandoned after an Indian attack killed several people at the fort. The survivors, including John Luttig and Lisette Charbonneau, fled down the Missouri River, arriving in St. Louis in late May. Because no one at the fort had seen Toussaint Charbonneau for several months, it was assumed that he had been killed.

John Luttig's journal entry recording the death of the wife of Charbonneau.

Believing Lisette and Pomp to be orphans, Luttig went to the St. Louis courthouse on August 11, 1813, to have himself appointed their legal guardian. William Clark was not in St. Louis at that time, but upon his return he replaced Luttig as guardian.

Word eventually came down the Missouri River that Toussaint Charbonneau was still alive. However, Sacagawea's husband allowed Clark to retain legal custody of the children. Aside from the adoption papers, there is no further record of Lisette. Most historians believe that Sacagawea's daughter died at a young age.

Jean Baptiste lived a long life. He grew up in St. Louis, where William Clark fulfilled his promise that Pomp

In the years following Sacagawea's death, the Shoshone woman's husband continued to work as a Hidatsa translator. Charbonneau appears in this 1834 lithograph by Karl Bodmer, who depicts himself (far right) and fellow traveler Prince Max von Wied-Neuwied (second from the right) being introduced to the Hidatsa Indians by the translator.

would receive an education. When the boy turned 18, he met German duke Paul Wilhelm of Baden-Wuerttemberg, who had come to America to collect Indian artifacts and plant and animal specimens. Pomp traveled with the duke to Europe, where he lived for six years, before returning to the United States in 1829.

Upon his return from Germany, Jean Baptiste worked as a fur trapper, scout, interpreter, and guide in various parts of the West. Later, he worked as a hotel clerk in California, before striking out for Montana to find his fortune as a gold miner. On May 16, 1866, on his way to the

Although presumed dead around the time of Sacagawea's death in 1812, Toussaint Charbonneau actually lived well into his eighties. He is thought to have died sometime between 1838 and 1843.

Sacagawea's Grandson

A historian doing research in the town where Pomp lived in Germany discovered the baptismal record of a boy named Anton Fries who was born on February 20, 1829. The document listed the infant's mother as Anastasia Katerina Fries and the father as Jean Baptiste Charbonneau of St. Louis, America. The child lived less than three months. No one can say for certain whether Pomp even knew he had fathered a child before he left Europe. He apparently never married or had any other children.

goldfields, the 61-year-old Jean-Baptiste died of pneumonia and was buried near Danner, Oregon.

ANOTHER THEORY

The place and date of Sacagawea's death is perhaps even more controversial than her name. In 1933, Grace Raymond Hebard, a professor at the University of Wyoming, published a book entitled *Sacajawea: Guide and Interpreter of Lewis and Clark*. In her book, Hebard proclaimed that Sacagawea did not die in 1812 at Fort Manuel, but in Wyoming in 1884.

According to Hebard, the woman described in Luttig's journal was one of Charbonneau's other wives and not Sacagawea. Instead, Hebard stated, Sacagawea left Charbonneau around that time and "drifted" to Comanche country on the southern Great Plains. She married a Comanche man, had several children with him, and eventually migrated north to Wyoming, where she and Pomp lived together into the late 1800s.

A marker commemorating the life of Sacagawea stands near the North Dakota-South Dakota border, close to the town of Kenel. (Her name appears in the official spelling used in North Dakota.) The marker lies close to the site of Fort Manuel, where most historians believe the Shoshone woman died in 1812. In 1978 the Fort Manuel site was placed on the National Register of Historic Places as the final resting place of Sacagawea.

Hebard had heard stories about an elderly Shoshone woman from Wyoming who had been familiar with the Lewis and Clark Expedition. The Shoshones had known her as Porivo, but Hebard determined that the Indian woman must have been Sacagawea. In researching her treatise, Hebard interviewed people who had known Porivo, including some who claimed to be her descendants.

However, today Hebard's research is considered faulty. For example, the death of Pomp in 1866 in Oregon is well documented—he didn't live with Sacagawea until the 1880s. Although historians have discredited Hebard's work, some people today continue to believe her version of Sacagawea's life and death are true.

After serving briefly as governor of the Louisiana Territory, Meriwether Lewis died at age 35 of gunshot wounds, possible self-inflicted, in 1809. William Clark married after the expedition and spent most of the rest of his life as a businessman and government official in St. Louis. He died in 1838, at age 69.

HER FINAL RESTING PLACE

John Luttig, the fur company clerk who recorded the death of "the wife of Charbonneau" and brought her daughter Lisette safely to St. Louis, was a former employee of William Clark. It is likely that Clark would have heard the story of Sacagawea's death at Fort Manuel from Luttig and from other witnesses.

In the 1820s, Clark wrote a list of the members of Corps of Discovery and added what he knew of their fate. "Se car ja we au," he wrote, was dead. Historian Donald Jackson notes that Clark would have good reason to be definite about the facts concerning the Charbonneau family:

> Sacagawea, Charbonneau, and her children were Clark's concern for many years after the Expedition. He cared about them and felt a kind of responsibility for them. It is difficult to believe he could have been wrong about Sacagawea's death.

But because Luttig wrote "the wife of Charbonneau" instead of the name *Sacagawea*, there will always be room for doubt.

10

REMEMBERING SACAGAWEA

In an August 20, 1806, letter that William Clark wrote to Toussaint Charbonneau, the captain acknowledged the debt the Lewis and Clark Expedition owed to Sacagawea:

> [Y]our woman who accompanied you that long dangerous and fatigueing rout to the Pacific Ocian and back diserved a greater reward for her attention and services on that rout than we had in our power to give her.

Unlike her husband, Sacagawea never received any money or land from the government as payment for her services.

"HER ATTENTION AND SERVICES"

During the long journey, Sacagawea provided support to the expedition that went well beyond the tasks of an interpreter. She was a supplier of food and medicine, gathering

Charbono

On Board the Perogue near the Ricara Village
August 20th 1806

Sir

Your present situation with the Indians gives me some concern — I wish now that I had advised you to come on with me to the Illinois where it most probably would be in my power to put you in some way to do something for your self — I was so engaged after the Big White had concluded to go down with Jessomme as his interpreter, that I had not time to talk with you as much as I intended to have done — You have been a long time with me and have conducted your self in such a manner as to gain my friendship, your woman who accompanied you that long dangerous and fatigueing rout to the Pacific Ocean and back, diserved a greater reward for her attention and services on that rout than we had in our power to give her at the Mandans as to your little son (my boy Pomp) you well know my fondness for him. and my anxiety to take and raise him as my own child. I once more tell you if you will bring your son Batteist to me I will educate him and treat him as my own child — I do not forget the promis which I made to you and shall now repeat them that you may be certain — Charbono, if you wish to live with the white people, and will come to me I will give you a piece of land and furnish you with horses cows & hogs — if you wish to visit your friends in Montreall I will let you have a horse, and your family shall be taken care of untill your return — if you wish to return as an Interpreter

In this letter by William Clark written after leaving the Knife River villages, the captain acknowledged to Charbonneau that the expedition owed much to the efforts of his wife, who "diserved a greater reward." Sacagawea received no monetary compensation for her contributions.

Sharing Her Knowledge

During the expedition, Lewis and Clark collected, preserved, and studied 176 plants that were unknown by scientists of the time, although long familiar to Native Americans. The journals reveal how Sacagawea frequently shared her knowledge about native plants with the Corps.

Serviceberry (*Amelanchier alnifolia*)
"Our interpreters Wife went on Shore & found great numver of fine berries, which is called service berries."
—Joseph Whitehouse, August 16, 1805

Wild Licorice (*Glycyrrhiza lepidota*)
"In walking on Shore with the Interpreter & his wife, the Squar Geathered on the Sides of the hills wild Lickerish, & the white apple."
—William Clark, May 8, 1805

native food and medicinal plants to supplement existing provisions. As a Native American, she served as a teacher for the members of the Corps, providing information about local plants and animals, as well as about the Indian culture of the Plains and Rockies.

In her role as Shoshone interpreter, Sacagawea was able to teach Lewis and Clark not only about her own people but also about several other tribes in which Shoshone speakers lived. As a result, Lewis and Clark were able communicate with words, rather than only sign language, and thus gain a good understanding of the cultures of various tribes.

Sacagawea made other important contributions to the expedition: She salvaged valuable papers, medicines, and baggage that had been knocked overboard during the trip up the Missouri River. She recognized landmarks that told the explorers they were on the right track, and when in familiar surroundings was able to point out paths they should travel.

Sacagawea was a young woman—still a teenager when she began the physically daunting task of journeying several thousand miles through familiar and unfamiliar lands. During that time, while giving her attention and service to the Corps of Discovery, she was also caring for her young son. The presence of the young mother and her child were an important symbol to the many Indian tribes the Lewis and Clark Expedition encountered. Since no war party would travel with women and children, it was obvious that the Corps had come in peace.

Flowers lie at the feet of the statue of a youthful Sacagawea. The Shoshone woman is remembered for her many contributions to the Lewis and Clark Expedition.

However, would the Lewis and Clark Expedition have failed without her? Her most important service was the one she had been hired to do: interpret Shoshone. She performed her role at a critical moment of the expedition: the portage of the Corps' belongings across the Continental Divide in August 1805. Sacagawea and Charbonneau helped persuade the Shoshone to help with this task and to lend horses for the effort. Once it was

During their 28-month journey, the Corps of Discovery came into contact with almost 50 different American native tribes. Most were friendly and hospitable, providing food, shelter, directions, and safe passage.

determined that the Corps would have to buy horses to continue their journey across the mountains, Sacagawea's service as an interpreter also aided in the bargaining.

And yet, the fact that Lewis did not take Sacagawea with him when he first set out to find the Shoshone suggests that he believed that he and the three men with him were capable on their own of persuading the Indians to help them. Nevertheless, the final agreements between the Shoshone and the leaders of the expedition did not take place until Sacagawea assumed her role as the group's interpreter and possibly influenced the decision with her presence and persuasive words.

SACAGAWEA'S LEGACY

The expedition did not produce the results that President Thomas Jefferson had hoped for. That is, Lewis and Clark did not discover a usable water route across North America. There is none. In addition, the expedition leaders did not convince the tribes encountered along the route to lay down their weapons and make peace with one another. War was an important a part of their cultures, and Lewis and Clark could not influence or change that reality.

But the expedition was successful in other ways. A major accomplishment was the recording of massive amounts of information that was eventually published and made available to the rest of the world. One of Sacagawea's greatest contribution to American history

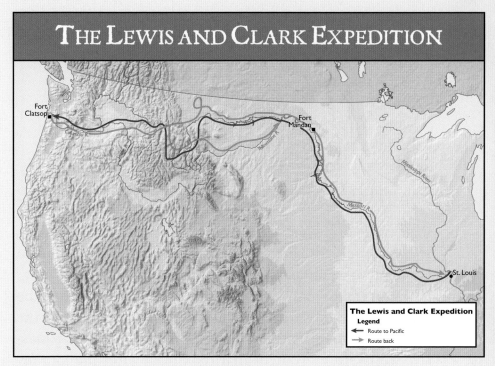

THE LEWIS AND CLARK EXPEDITION

The Lewis and Clark Expedition
Legend
← Route to Pacific
→ Route back

Because the Lewis and Clark Expedition followed the meandering Missouri and Columbia River systems, the journey from St. Louis to the Pacific coast and back covered nearly 8,000 miles. Sacagawea, carrying her young son, accompanied the expedition for an estimated 4,356 of those miles.

was her patient interpretation for Lewis and Clark of her own Shoshone culture and of those of other tribes such as the Nez Perce, Salish, and Walla Walla. Up until then, these tribes had had little contact with Euro-Americans and very little was known about their cultures.

The members of the Corps were the first whites to record their impressions and, in some cases, it would be many years before further studies were done. In 1805 and 1806, Sacagawea, Charbonneau and the French interpreters of the Corps, Lewis, Clark and other members of the Corps of Discovery worked as a team to record and preserve priceless portraits of American cultures—societies

The Hidatsa village Awatixa, where Sacagawea lived with her husband, is now known as the Sakakawea Site. Located near Stanton, North Dakota, it is part of the Knife River Indian Villages National Historic Site, administered by the U.S. National Park Service. Near Sacagawea's Shoshone homeland of Idaho is a 71-acre park known as the Sacajawea Interpretive, Cultural, and Educational Center, which is owned and operated by the city of Salmon.

that within a few generations would all but vanish. Thanks to Sacagawea, we know much more about American Indian life than we would have without her.

However, to many Native Americans, the success of the Lewis and Clark Expedition marked the beginning of the end of their traditional way of life. As a result of the massive westward movement that took place after the journey of the Corps ended, Native Americans were killed by new diseases brought by whites and by warfare with them. Many tribes lost their homelands and were forced to move onto reservations. Their way of life ended with the opening up of the West to Euro-Americans.

HONORING SACAGAWEA

The woman who helped guide and interpret for the Lewis and Clark Expedition is remembered today as a symbol of strength and character. She has been honored by the U.S. government in many ways—numerous statues of Sacagawea can be found across the United States, and mountain peaks, rivers, and lakes have been named for her. In 1999, the U.S. Mint unveiled the gold-colored dollar coin that bears a representative image of her. The first Sacagawea dollars were released in 2000.

Journals of the Louis and Clark Expedition

The journal of Sergeant Patrick Gass was the first from the Louis and Clark Expedition to be published, in 1807. Lewis and Clark's journals, edited by Nicholas Biddle and Paul Allen and with a preface written by Thomas Jefferson, appeared in 1814. This account also included information from journals by Sergeants Gass and Ordway.

Sacagawea would not receive much recognition in published stories about the Lewis and Clark Expedition until 1893, when another version of the journals, edited by Elliot Coues, appeared. His enthusiastic depictions of her contributions to the Corps made her a household name.

Sacagawea was never formally hired by the captains or given government recognition as a member of the expedition. However, on January 18, 2001, when President Bill Clinton granted posthumous promotions to members of the Lewis and Clark Expedition, he granted Sacagawea the title of honorary sergeant in the regular army. "She is," said Amy Mossett, director of tourism for the Mandan, Hidatsa and Arikara tribes, "the most celebrated woman in American history."

First minted in 2000, the gold-colored Sacagawea dollar coin honors the Shoshone woman who shared her culture with the explorers from the east and who helped make the Lewis and Clark Expedition a success.

CHRONOLOGY

Circa 1788   Sacagawea is born into the Shoshone tribe, in the Lemhi River Valley of Idaho.

1800   Hidatsa raiders kidnap Sacagawea at the Three Forks of Missouri, in Montana. They take her to live at the Knife River villages in present-day North Dakota.

1803   In April, French emperor Napoleon agrees to sell the Louisiana Territory to the United States for $15 million. President Thomas Jefferson recruits Captains Meriwether Lewis and William Clark to explore the territory of Louisiana, with the goal of finding a waterway to the Pacific Ocean. In December, the Lewis and Clark Expedition builds Camp River Dubois near St. Louis, Missouri, where expedition recruits are trained.

1803 or 1804   French-Canadian trader Toussaint Charbonneau obtains Sacagawea from the Hidatsa and makes her his wife.

1804   On May 14, the expedition leaves Camp River Dubois and heads north up the Missouri River. In October, it arrives at the Knife River villages, in present-day North Dakota. In November, Lewis and Clark hire Charbonneau to interpret Hidatsa, and he and Sacagawea move to the Corps' winter quarters, Fort Mandan.

1805   In February, Sacagawea gives birth to Jean Baptiste Charbonneau. The following April, the expedition continues its journey up the Missouri River, accompanied by Sacagawea, Charbonneau, and their child. In May, Sacagawea saves valuable cargo during a boat accident; Lewis and Clark name a river for her. After traveling the upper forks of the Missouri, the expedition reaches the navigable limits of the Jefferson River in mid-August. Sacagawea is reunited with her Shoshone tribe. She serves as an interpreter in a council in which the Shoshone agree to provide horses and guides to the expedition. In September, the Corps of Discovery crosses the Bitterroot Mountains to the Clearwater River in present-day northern Idaho. After building canoes, they continue their westward journey in October, following the Clearwater, Snake, and Columbia Rivers. Members of the expedition sight the Pacific Ocean on November 7, 1805. In December, near the Oregon coast, they build Fort Clatsop.

1806 In March, Sacagawea and the rest of the Corps set out for the journey home via the Columbia River system. The expedition crosses the Bitterroots in late June and in early July separates as Lewis's party travels to the northeast. Sacagawea travels southeast, with Clark's party, to explore the Yellowstone River; after recognizing familiar landmarks, she guides the group through Bozeman Pass to the Yellowstone. On August 12, members of the expedition reunite; five days later they arrive back at the Knife River villages, and Sacagawea and Charbonneau leave the expedition; Lewis and Clark reach St. Louis on September 23.

1809 The Charbonneau family arrives in St. Louis to receive the additional pay and land grant awarded by Congress to Charbonneau and the other members of the Corps.

1811 Charbonneau accepts an interpreter's job with a fur company; he and Sacagawea travel up the Missouri River, but leave their son

Jean Baptiste behind in St. Louis to attend school.

1812   Charbonneau, Sacagawea, and an infant daughter, Lisette, arrive at Fort Manuel, a fur trading post on the Missouri River, near present-day Kenel, South Dakota. On December 12, a fur trader named John Luttig records in his journal that Sacagawea has died.

Circa 1843   Touissant Charbonneau dies.

1866   Sacagawea's son, Jean Baptiste "Pompy" Charbonneau, dies in Oregon.

1884   The death in Wyoming, on the Wind River Shoshoni Reservation, of an Indian woman some people believe to have been Sacagawea.

1906   The first statue of Sacagawea is unveiled during the centennial celebration of the Lewis and Clark Expedition, in Portland, Oregon.

1999   In November, the U.S. Mint unveils the new Sacagawea dollar coin, which is first circulated in 2000.

2007   Congress approves a new design of the Sacagawea dollar that will feature the Shoshone woman on one side and various Indian tribes and other Native Americans on the reverse side.

CHAPTER NOTES

Chapter 1: Who Was Sacagawea?

p. 14   "This is the first time . . ." Lisa Blee, "Completing Lewis and Clark's Westward March: Exhibiting a History of Empire at the 1905 Portland's World Fair," *Oregon Historical Quarterly*, Summer 2005, p. 22. http://www.historycooperative.org/journals/ohq/106.2/blee.html

Chapter 2: A Shoshone Girl

p. 24   "Our present camp . . ." Gary Moulton, ed., *The Journals of the Lewis and Clark Expedition*, Volume 5. Lincoln: University of Nebraska Press, 1988, pp. 8–9.

Chapter 3: The Lewis and Clark Expedition

p. 32   "The object of your mission . . ." Donald Jackson, ed., *Letters of the Lewis and Clark Expedition with Related Documents 1783–1854*, Volume 1. Urbana: University of Illinois Press, 1978, p. 61.

p. 35   "are verry troublesome." Reuben Gold Thwaites, ed., *Original Journals of the Lewis and Clark Expedition: 1804–1806*, Volume I. New York: Dodd, Mead & Company, 1904, p. 51.

p. 40   "a shot was fired . . ." Carol Lynn MacGregor, *The Journals of Patrick Gass*. Missoula, Montana: Mountain Press Publishing Company, 1997, p. 74.

p. 40   "You will . . . endeavor to make . . ." Jackson, *Letters of the Lewis and Clark Expedition*, p. 62.

Chapter 4: The Shoshone "Interpretress"

p. 43   "a Mr. Chaubonée, interpeter . . ." Moulton, *The Journals of the Lewis and Clark Expedition*, Volume 3. Lincoln: University of Nebraska Press, 1987, p. 228.

p. 44   "[A] clear and pleasant morning." Milo M. Quaife, *The Journals of Captain Meriwether Lewis and Sergeant John Ordway*. Madison, Wisconsin: The State Historical Society of Wisconsin, 1916, p. 136.

pp. 45–46 "about five oclock this evening . . ." Moulton, *The Journals of the Lewis and Clark Expedition*, Volume 3. p. 291.

p. 46   "tedious and the pain violent . . ." Moulton, *The Journals of the Lewis and Clark Expedition*, Volume 3, p. 291.

p. 46   "small portion of the rattle . . ." Moulton, *The Journals of the Lewis and Clark Expedition*, Volume 3, p. 291.

p. 46   "I must confess . . ." Moulton, *The Journals of the Lewis and Clark Expedition*, Volume 3, p. 291.

p. 49   "Shabonah [Charbonneau] and his Indian Squar . . ." Thwaites, *Original Journals of the Lewis and Clark Expedition: 1804–1806*, Volume 1, p. 287.

Chapter 5: Seeking the Headwaters of the Missouri

p. 51   "The woman that is with us . . ." MacGregor, *The Journals of Patrick Gass*, p. 86.

p. 52   "[W]hen we halted for dinner . . ." Moulton, *The Journals of the Lewis and Clark Expedition*, Volume 4. Lincoln: University of Nebraska Press, 1987, p. 15.

p. 53   "bore delicious froot . . . " Moulton, *The Journals of the Lewis and Clark Expedition*, Volume 4, p. 89.

p. 54   "in short . . . almost every article . . ." Moulton, *The Journals of the Lewis and Clark Expedition*, Volume 4, p. 152.

p. 54   "[W]e therefore hoisted both the sails . . ." Moulton, *The Journals of the Lewis and Clark Expedition*, Volume 4, p. 29.

p. 55   "[T]his accedent was very near . . ." Moulton, *The Journals of the Lewis and Clark Expedition*, Volume 4, p. 29.

p. 55   "would most probably have perished . . ." Moulton, *The Journals of the Lewis and Clark Expedition*, Volume 4, p. 30.

p. 55   "The Indian woman to whom . . ." Moulton, *The Journals of the Lewis and Clark Expedition*, Volume 5, p. 157.

p. 56   "[A]bout five miles above the mouth of shell river . . ." Reuben Gold Thwaites, ed., *Original Journals of the Lewis and Clark Expedition: 1804–1806*, Volume II. New York: Dodd, Mead & Company, 1904, p. 52

p. 57   "[O]ur Intrepters wife verry Sick," Quaife, *The Journals of Captain Meriwether Lewis and Sergeant John Ordway*, p. 202.

p. 58   "The bier in which the woman . . ." Thwaites, *Original Journals of the Lewis and Clark Expedition: 1804–1806*, Volume II, pp. 197–198.

p. 59   "her pulse were scarcely perceptible . . ." Moulton, *The Journals of the Lewis and Clark Expedition*, Volume 4, p. 300.

p. 59   "At breakfast our squaw . . ." MacGregor, *The Journals of Patrick Gass*, p. 112.

p. 60   "The bottom of the River . . ." Quaife, *The Journals of Captain Meriwether Lewis and Sergeant John Ordway*, p. 230.

Chapter 6: Finding Sacagawea's People

p. 61   "The Indian woman recognized . . ." Moulton, *The Journals of the Lewis and Clark Expedition*, Volume 5, p. 59.

p. 63   "[I]t is now all important . . ." Gary Moulton, ed., *The Journals of the Lewis and Clark Expedition*, Volume 5, p. 59.

p. 64   "The men Complain much of their fatigue . . ." Moulton, *The Journals of the Lewis and Clark Expedition*, Volume 5, p. 100.

p. 64   "I have no accounts . . ." Moulton, *The Journals of the Lewis and Clark Expedition*, Volume 5, p. 100.

p. 65   "[A] clear cold morning . . ." Quaife, *The Journals of Captain Meriwether Lewis and Sergeant John Ordway*, p. 239.

p. 65   "There were about 20 . . ." MacGregor, *The Journals of Patrick Gass*, p. 118.

p. 66   "I had mentioned to the chief . . ." Thwaites, *Original Journals of the Lewis and Clark Expedition: 1804–1806*, Volume II, p. 358.

p. 67   "[A]bout 4 P. M we called them together . . ." Thwaites, *Original Journals of the Lewis and Clark Expedition: 1804–1806*, Volume II, p. 362.

p. 69   "immence ranges of high mountains . . ." Moulton, *The Journals of the Lewis and Clark Expedition*, Volume 5, p. 74.

Chapter 7: On to the Pacific

p. 73   "[A]ltho' [Charbonneau] had been in possession . . ." Moulton, *The Journals of the Lewis and Clark Expedition*, Volume 5, p. 165.

p. 75   "[W]e passed a nomber of large Springs . . ." Quaife, *The Journals of Captain Meriwether Lewis and Sergeant John Ordway*, p. 246.

p. 77   "I have been wet . . ." Moulton, *The Journals of the Lewis and Clark Expedition*, Volume 5, p. 209.

p. 77   "[The Nez Perce] gave us a Small piece of Buffalow meat . . ." Moulton, *The Journals of the Lewis and Clark Expedition*, Volume 5, p. 222.

p. 81   "The wife of Shabono . . ." Moulton, *The Journals of the Lewis and Clark Expedition*, Volume 5, p. 268.

Chapter 8: Waiting Out the Winter

p. 83   "Janey in favour . . ." Gary Moulton, ed., *The Journals of the Lewis and Clark Expedition*, Volume 6, Lincoln: University of Nebraska Press, 1990, p. 84.

p. 84   "[O]ne of the Indians had on a roab . . ." Moulton, *The Journals of the Lewis and Clark Expedition*, Volume 6, pp. 72–73.

p. 84   "A Coate of Blue cloth," Moulton, *The Journals of the Lewis and Clark Expedition*, Volume 6, p. 73.

p. 84   "They have found a place . . ." MacGregor, *The Journals of Patrick Gass*, p. 156.

p. 85   "Captain Clark and his men . . ." Patrick Gass and James Kendall Hosmer, *Gass's Journal of the Lewis and Clark Expedition*. A. C. McClurg & Co., 1904, p. 76.

p. 86   "Shabono and his Indian woman . . ." Moulton, *The Journals of the Lewis and Clark Expedition*, Volume 6, p. 171.

p. 87   "Steepest worst and highest mountain . . ." Moulton, *The Journals of the Lewis and Clark Expedition*, Volume 6, p. 176.

p. 91   "[W]e found a Shoshone woman . . ." Gary Moulton, ed., *The Journals of the Lewis and Clark Expedition*, Volume 7, Lincoln: University of Nebraska Press, 1991, p. 178.

p. 92   "very agreeable food . . ." Moulton, ed., *The Journals of the Lewis and Clark Expedition*, Volume 7, p. 264.

p. 93   "I took my leave . . ." Gary Moulton, ed., *The Journals of the Lewis and Clark Expedition*, Volume 8, Lincoln: University of Nebraska Press, 1993, p. 161.

Chapter 9: "A Pilot Through This Country"

p. 95   "[W]e assended a Small rise . . ." Gary E. Moulton, ed. *The Definitive Journals of Lewis and Clark: Over the Rockies to St. Louis*, Volume 8. : Lincoln, Neb.: Bison Books, 2002, p. 167.

p. 95   "[O]ur Intrepters wife tells us . . ." Quaife, *The Journals of Captain Meriwether Lewis and Sergeant John Ordway*, p. 345.

p. 96   "[Sacagawea] recognised the plain immediately. . . ." John Back McMaster, Nicholas Biddle, ed. *History of the Expedition Under the Command of Captains Lewis & Clarke*, Volume 3. New York: Allerton Book Company, 1902, p. 208.

p. 97 "[T]he indian woman . . ." Gary Moulton, ed., *The Journals of the Lewis and Clark Expedition*, Volume 8, p. 180.

p. 98 "We also took our leave . . ." Moulton, *The Journals of the Lewis and Clark Expedition*, Volume 8, p. 305.

p. 99 "little Son," Moulton, *The Journals of the Lewis and Clark Expedition*, Volume 8, p. 305.

p. 99 "a butifull promising Child . . ." Moulton, *The Journals of the Lewis and Clark Expedition*, Volume 8, p. 305.

p. 99 "in Such a manner . . ." Moulton, *The Journals of the Lewis and Clark Expedition*, Volume 8, pp. 305–6.

p. 102 "As to your little Son . . ." Jackson, *Letters of the Lewis and Clark Expedition*, Volume 1, p. 315.

p. 103 "become weary of civilized life," Henry M. Brackenridge, *Views of Louisiana, Together with a Journal of a Voyage up the Missouri River in 1811*. Pittsburgh: Cramer, Spear and Eichbaum, 1814, p. 202.
http://www.xmission.com/~drudy/mtman/html/Brackenridge/Brackenridge.html

p. 103 "The woman . . . of a mild and gentle disposition. . ." Henry M. Brackenridge, *Views of Louisiana, Together with a Journal of a Voyage up the Missouri River in 1811*, p. 202.

p. 104 "This evening the wife . . ." John C. Luttig, *Journal of a Fur-trading Expedition on the Upper Missouri 1812–1813*. St. Louis: Missouri Historical Society, 1920.
http://www.xmission.com/~drudy/mtman/html/Luttig/luttig.html

p. 109 "Sacagawea, Charbonneau, and her children . . ." Colton Storm, ed. *A Catalogue of the Everett D. Graff Collection of Western Americana*. Chicago, Ill.: University of Chicago Press, 1968, p. 118.

Chapter 10: Remembering Sacagawea

p. 110   "[Y]our woman who accompanied you . . ." Jackson, *Letters of the Lewis and Clark Expedition*, p. 315.

p. 112   "Our interpreters Wife went on Shore . . ." Lewis as Botanist.
http://www.lewisandclarktrail.com/nativeplants.htm

p. 112   "In walking on Shore with the Interpreter . . ." Moulton, *The Journals of the Lewis and Clark Expedition*, Volume 4, p. 128.

p. 117   "She is the most celebrated . . ." "Sacagawea Famed, Yet a Mystery: Interpreter's Role Central to Bicentennial Commemoration of Lewis and Clark," *Washington Post*, December 30, 2002.

GLOSSARY

asperity—harshness or roughness.

confluence—junction of two equal-sized rivers.

divide—a ridge or area of high ground that separates two river systems. The Continental Divide in North America separates the headwaters of the Missouri river system, which flows east and south into the Gulf of Mexico, from the Columbia river system, which flows west to the Pacific Ocean.

eddy—circular movement of water forming a small whirlpool.

estuary—the mouth of a river where freshwater meets the incoming tides of saltwater from the sea or ocean.

Great Basin—a geographical region that includes most of Nevada and western Utah.

headwaters—the tributary streams and rivers that are the source of a larger river.

keelboat—a large flat-bottomed riverboat used for carrying freight in shallow water.

meander—to follow a winding or indirect route.

opium—an addictive drug made from a species of poppy; used to relieve pain.

Peruvian bark—the bark from a South American tree from which the drug quinine is derived; used to treat malaria.

petroglyph—rock carving.

pilot—guide.

pirogue—large rowboat used to carry freight on rivers.

portage—the practice of carrying baggage or boats overland between two navigable rivers or around an obstacle in a river.

poultice—a soft, warm mixture applied to a part of the body for medical purposes.

riffle—a shallow, rocky part of a stream or river.

tributary—a stream or river that flows into a larger river.

venison—the meat from a game animal, especially a deer.

vermilion—a bright red pigment that comes from the mineral cinnabar (mercury sulfide); it was one of the paints carried by the Lewis and Clark Expedition as a gift for the Indians.

watershed—the area of land in which waters drain into a larger river or body of water.

FURTHER READING

Books for Students:

Fradin, Judith Bloom, et al. *Who Was Sacagawea?* New York: Grosset & Dunlap, 2002.

Meyer, R. Jane. *The Adventures of Sacagawea.* Great Falls, Mont.: Lewis and Clark Interpretive Association, 2001.

Roop, Connie, and Peter Roop. *Sacagawea: Girl of the Shining Mountains.* New York: Hyperion Books for Children, 2003.

Thomasma, Ken. *The Truth About Sacajawea.* Jackson, Wyo.: Grandview Publishing, 1997.

Tinling, Marion. *Sacagawea's Son.* Missoula, Mont.: Mountain Press Publishing Company, 2001.

Wallner, Rosemary. *Sacagawea: 1788–1812.* Mankato, Minn.: Blue Earth Books, 2003.

White, Alana J. *Sacagawea: West with Lewis and Clark.* Berkeley Heights, N.J.: Enslow Publishers, 1997.

Books for Older Readers:

Ambrose, Stephen. *Undaunted Courage.* New York: Simon and Schuster, 1996.

Howard, Harold P. *Sacajawea.* Norman, Okla.: University of Oklahoma Press, 1971.

Hunsaker, Joyce Badgeley. *Sacagawea Speaks: Beyond the Shining Mountains with Lewis and Clark.* Guilford, Conn. and Helena, Mont.: 2001.

Kessler, Donna. *The Making of Sacagawea: The Making of a Euro-American Legend.* Tuscaloosa, Ala.: University of Alabama Press, 1996.

Madsen, Brigham D. *The Lemhi: Sacajawea's People.* Caldwell, Idaho: Caxton Printers, 1979, 2000.

Moulton, Gary, ed. *The Journals of the Lewis and Clark Expedition,* Volumes 3–11. Lincoln, Neb.: University of Nebraska Press, 1987–1997.

Reid, Russell. *Sakakawea, The Bird Woman.* Bismarck: State Historical Society of North Dakota, 1986.

INTERNET RESOURCES

http://sacajawea.idahostatesman.com/

Sponsored by the newspaper *Idaho Statesman*, this Sacajawea website contains a collection of oral tradition stories based on interviews with descendants of the Lemhi Shoshone.

http://l3.ed.uidaho.edu/index.asp?ExpeditionID=1

The Lewis and Clark Re-Discovery Project is sponsored by the University of Idaho and organized from both the Euro-American and American Indian perspective. Major locations associated with the expedition are discussed under six subtopics: the expedition, culture, geography, people, maps, and nature.

http://www.lewisandclark200.org/index_nf.php?cID=

This official National Lewis and Clark Bicentennial website gives detailed information on American Indian tribes, reached through the link "American Indian Nations." Other subtopics include Care for the Land and Water, Travel the Trail, Learn About the Journey, and Students and Teachers.

http://www.lewisclarkandbeyond.com/mainPage/

Lewis, Clark and Beyond is a National Park Service website consisting of three sections: "Education" features lesson plans and journal excerpts, "Bicentennial" covers the route of Corps of Discovery II, a traveling National Park Service exhibit and performance program that appeared across the United States during the expedition's 200 year anniversary. "Corps II" features more than 900 videos.

http://lewisandclarkjournals.unl.edu/

> The *Journals of the Lewis and Clark Expedition*, as edited by Gary Moulton, can be accessed here, along with articles, maps, images, and audio and video presentations.

http://www.lewis-clark.org/

> This *Discovering Lewis and Clark* website was produced by Joseph Mussulman of the University of Montana with the help of leading Lewis and Clark scholars. Major topics include The Expedition, American Nation, The Corps, Geography, Native Nations, and Natural History.

INDEX

Numbers in **bold italics** refer to captions.

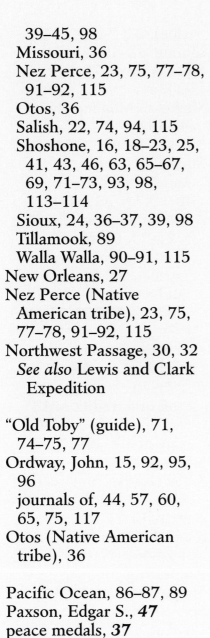

PICTURE CREDITS

Michael Crosby was born in Giessen, Germany, in 1950, and has lived in Salmon, Idaho since 1974 with his wife Candace. Michael was a teacher and counselor in the Salmon schools from 1974 to 2000. He earned an M.A. in American history at the University of Idaho in 1983.

Mr. Crosby was voted the Salmon Teacher of the Year in 1980, received the Teaching Excellence Award by the University of Idaho Alumni Association in 1983, and was the state winner of the "Take Pride in Idaho" award for history education in 1990. He has taught summer school and extension courses for the University of Idaho, Ricks College, and Idaho State University.

In 2000 Mr. Crosby joined the Bureau of Land Management in Salmon as interpretive historian for the Lewis and Clark Bicentennial, and worked during the summer months at Lemhi Pass and at the Sacajawea Interpretive Center in Salmon. He also appeared at Lewis and Clark Signature Events, beginning in 2003 at Charlottesville, Virginia, and ending in 2006 at St. Louis, Missouri. From 2001 to 2006 more than 10 thousand people attended Mr. Crosby's interpretive programs. On August 12, 2005, Mr. Crosby portrayed Private Hugh McNeal in the Bicentennial reenactment of the arrival of the Corps of Discovery at Lemhi Pass.

During the Bicentennial Mr. Crosby published a weekly Lewis and Clark article in the Salmon *Recorder-Herald* and on the Bureau of Land Management's website.

His previous books are *I'd Do It Again in a Minute! The History of the Civilian Conservation Corps on the Salmon National Forest* and *Joined by a Journey: The Lives of the Lewis and Clark Corps of Discovery*. He is currently working on a biography of Sacagawea for adults.